THE FRENCH RIVIERA

Introduction by
ALAIN DECAUX
of the French Academy

Text by
JEAN VALBONNE

Translated by
DAVID MACRAE

Minerva

Credits : Beck/Vloo : 75b — Ber/Atlas : 11b — Berne/Fotogram : 64b, 69b — Boutin/Vloo : 55b, 56c, 57b, 60a, 61a, 65a, 66, 71a, 74d, 80b — Charles/Atlas : 12a, b, 18b — Chaveyron/Atlas : 21a — Clasen/Vloo : 45a, 54b — Corniglion/ Atlas : 25a, 33b, 39b, 41a, 42a, b, c, d, e, 43b, 44a — Corte/Vloo : 53a — Damm/Zefa : 70 — Degeorges/Atlas : 49a — Fiore : 7, 9a, 10b, 11a, 19a, 20c, 26a — Frederick/Atlas : 19b — Freret/Atlas : 10a — Froissardey/Atlas : 15b, 16a, b, 17a, b, 21c, 27a, b, c, 56b, 89b — Garbison/Fotogram : 48c — Geay/Lauros : 69a — Gérard/Fotogram : 48b — d'Heilly/Atlas : 8b — Houdebine/Atlas : 28b — Hureau/Atlas : 38b, 40b, 84b, 86, 88a, 90a, 91, 95b — Jean-Pierre/ Vloo : 8a — Laitier/Vloo : 13a — Lauros : 56a — Lauros/Atals : 15a, 51a — Lavalette/Vloo : 29b — Lecron/Atlas : 24b, 25b — Lenars/Atlas : 24a, 61b, 63a, b, 75d, 76 — Lepage/Vloo : 77a — Leprohon : 1, 2, 3, 4, 20b, 22, 30, 32, 33c, 34a, b, 35c, 38a, 40a, 41b, c, 43a, 44b, 45b, c, 46a, b, c, 48a, 49c, 50a, 52b, 54a, c, d, 55a, 56c, d, 57a, 58a, b, c, 60b, 62a, 68a, b, e, f, 71b, 75c, 76a, c, 78b, 80a, c, 82a, 83a, 88b, 90b, c, 94c, 95a — N. Leser : 45c — Loucel/Atlas : 62b, 68c, d, g — Mangiavaca/Vloo : 33a, 35b — Mathieu/Atlas : end papers — Messerschmidt/Vloo : 36, 76b, 78a — Momy/Atlas : 21b — Monferrant/Vloo : 53b — Nestgen /Atlas : 6 — Pavard/Fotogram : 64a — Petit/Atlas : 9b, 13b, 14a, 28c, 29a, 51b, 52a, 53c, 55d, 74c — Putatti/Vloo : 75a, 84a — Rial/Atlas : 20a, 26b, 28a, 39a, 81, 89a, c — Soriano/Atlas : 65b, 94a, b — Soro/Atlas : 92 — Spectrum/Vloo : 49b — Valarcher/Atlas : 55c, 59b, 82b, 83b, 85a, b, c, d, e — Vieil/ Vloo : 18a — Volka/Atlas : 35a — Watteau/Vloo : 59a, 72, 74a, b, 77b, 79 — Yolka/Atlas : 14b.

Designed and produced by Editions Minerva SA,

© Editions Minerva SA, Genève, 1982

ISBN 0-517-351137

Printed in Italy

In 1763, Tobias George Smollet was forty years old. This eminent Scot was a renowned and prolific writer; his complete works, published in London in 1895, filled no less than twenty volumes. Without a doubt, the most curious of his works is that entitled *The History and Adventures of an Atom*. Smollet had even translated Voltaire into English. Besides five volumes on the history of England, he also wrote *Travels through France and Italy,* which contains a description of the town, region and climate of Nice. It was these two volumes, published in London in 1766, that really "launched" the French Riviera.

In those days it took 7½ days to get from Calais to Lyon, three days from Lyon to Avignon and four days from Avignon to Nice. Between Calais and Paris there were 27 relay stations, and another 80 from Paris to the Var. Each of them meant a long wait in insipid surroundings, with compulsory tips. A bitterly resentful Smollet paid out a total of one hundred and twenty pounds—a fortune in those days. It is therefore not surprising that he took an increasingly dim view of everything around him as he moved southwards. The roads were bad, the inns appalling. Most of the time he was refused a single room, and found himself sleeping in makeshift dormitories with strangers who snored or reeked of garlic—a smell with which few Scots were then familiar. He went through Cannes, which was then just a small fishing town, beyond Antibes, across the Loup on a new bridge and then came to the Var. Eventually he arranged to be taken to the other side, having parted with a fat tip to the boatmen. Yet at this point, our dour traveler's stony face broke into a smile: he had just begun to experience the climatic shock which has delighted so many millions of travelers since then.

He was astonished to find that, although it was still midwinter, with frost on the ground at dawn, the sun was as warm as it would normally be in England in May.

Smollet spent two winters in Nice, where he wrote abundantly. He found fault with everything. His impression was that the maids were lazy, negligent and revoltingly dirty, and the streets of Nice were full of dung. The shopkeepers were grasping and fraudulent, while the craftsmen and workers thought of nothing but lounging about in the sun. The doctors charged exorbitant fees, as much as six pence per visit; however, as Smollett casually observed, one could manage not to pay them.

Paradoxically, his criticism placed Nice firmly on the map. This was because Smollett, despite his evident reluctance to do so, could not withhold his joy. The fact that it rained so little particularly delighted him. He found the countryside enchanting, with its trees which stayed green in winter, its scented orange and lemon groves, and its olive trees. He strolled through fields of carnations, became acquainted with the local food, wholeheartedly approved of anchovies fried in oil and was beside himself with delight over water melons. He swore that the wine of Languedoc and the sweet wine of Saint-Laurent-du-Var were quite as good as Burgundy and Frontignan. He discovered a local brandy which he seems to have consumed to excess from time to time. And then, to the general amazement of the inhabitants of Nice, he went bathing in the sea: everyone was most surprised when they saw him bathing early in May. They found it odd to see a consumptive diving into the sea. But when it became evident that his health was improving as a result of his bathing, they started to imitate him. With the exception of the ladies, however. Smollett claims—in a nice implied tribute to the passionate temperament of the males of Nice—that if they had gone into the sea, lightly clad, they would have been exposed to such risks that they would have had to be accompanied by guards...

In the years which followed Smollett's visits the English came to Nice in ever larger numbers. In the mid-18th century there were only two hotels, the Hôtel de la Ville, and the Hôtel des Quatre Nations. They very soon proved inadequate. The English rented houses, costing up to one hundred and thirty pounds, for the whole winter. Then a large hotel, the Hôtel d'Angleterre, was built. Until the Revolution the English community in Nice included Lord and Lady Cavendish, Lady Fitzgerald, the Duke of York, brother of George III, the Duke and Duchess of Cumberland, the Duke of Bedford, Lord Bessborough, Lady Mynar and Lady Penelope Rivers. All of them felt the same sense of wonder at the Nice winters, which were so like the summers back home. Mary Harcourt, for one, was overwhelmed by the beauty of the place: she never tired of riding her donkey up and down the scented hills which stretch away inland behind Nice, picking the roses, carnations or the other flowers which she found on every bush, admiring the great eucalyptus trees and roaming aimlessly through the olive groves all the way down to the blue sea. She felt she was truly in a land of dreams.

Nice began to change, as far as the eye could see: fine residences were built for the unexpected guests, and a long terrace was laid out along the sea front, where the high society of Nice used to stroll.

Less than two centuries later (after numerous memorable and always colorful episodes) the Riviera was to be discovered a second time...

This was certainly the most fabulous phenomenon in the history of tourism. In less than ten years it recovered not only its clientèle from between the wars, but doubled, then tripled and finally quintupled it. At the Palm Beach, Jack Warner tossed million-franc plaques onto the green baize tables with breezy nonchalance. At the Sporting Club de Monaco, Darryl Zannuck would agree to interrupt his triumphant progress against the bank only if it was four o'clock. Mr. Onassis anchored his yacht at Monaco. The môme Moineau, a noted showbiz eccentric, preferred Cannes, while the Opel family had a soft spot for Saint-Tropez.

For the first time, moreover, hundreds of thousands of middle-income employees began to descend on the Riviera, quite as eager as the rich to enjoy the sun and the warm sea. Steering well clear of the grander hotels they sought out the "studios, 1-2 rms., water, gas, elec., reas. prices". Many others favored camping. The smallest vacant lot, the humblest pine grove were avidly hunted down.

Apartment blocks sprouted up all along the shore. Building speculation made fortunes for illiterate masons and imaginative architects. Starting one's own real estate agency was a sure way to strike it rich in five years. In the hinterland, the plainest little shanty was given a coat of ochre, advertised as a *mas* and sold within a month.

The key word was "to launch", in respect of places. A kind of symbiosis came into existence between the new and the old—between promoters and artists. By discovering the techniques of the potters of pre-history at Vallauris, Picasso gave the place renewed life as a resort. Henri-Georges Clouzot did a great deal for Saint-Paul-de-Vence. With a "Son et Lumière", André Castelot made many people aware, for the first time, of the Lérins Islands. Chapels were also much in vogue: Matisse at Vence and Cocteau at Villefranche made offerings to this cultural necessity which, apart from anything else, was very good for business.

Large numbers of civil servants and officers went to live on the Riviera. The *département* of Alpes-Maritimes pays out more retirement pensions than any other in the whole of France. It has been suggested, rather unkindly, that if all the retired generals and colonels in Nice were to go down into the streets in uniform, everyone would think that the 1914 war had been declared again.

There is a third category of people who have done much to bring the extremes closer together: the artists. Movie stars, music-hall singers, popular writers have also moved in on the Riviera, giving resorts like Saint-Tropez and Juan-les-Pins a new face, though not one which is to everyone's liking.

A huge city—that is what the French Riviera has now become. A city which runs for eighty miles along the sea, from Les Maures to the Italian frontiers. It is still dotted with plenty of green spaces, though they are shrinking with each passing year. Its districts are called Saint-Raphaël, Cannes, Juan, Antibes, Nice, Villefranche, Monte-Carlo and Menton. It is a city with a population density of 81,920 per square mile, or forty times higher than the average for France. And it is becoming increasingly dense, at a prodigious rate.

The sense of wonderment felt by Smollett is quite as acute when experienced by several million people. Nothing will be able to destroy the tremendous thrill of the moment when the visitor first sees the colors of the Riviera coast. Seen from a train window or through a car windshield, they are always striking. The rocks are too red, the sky too blue, the sea too dark and the trees too green. But it is an enchanting shock.

The warm water rolls the pebbles on the beach and spills the sand before it. The midday sun burns one's back. Like the colors, the sun also is aggressive, but at the same time gentle.

The history of the French Riviera reflects a constant desire man has always had, a need for a certain kind of light which is associated with happiness. Is it, after all, so strange that the loves of so many great people have taken place in this setting? Or that the ailing Marie Bashkirtseff, seeing the soft, ethereal silver-blue of the sky, knew that she had at last found happiness? The light is the same; and the happiness has been democratized.

ALAIN DECAUX
of the French Academy

A BOUQUET OF BEAUTIES

The name Côte d'Azur, by which the French Riviera is most commonly known in France, was first used by Stephen Liégeard, a politician and poet of the latter part of the 19th century. It soon became evident that his choice of words had been most successful.

It reflected a reality which was both physical and spiritual. It is true that nowhere else in France is the sky quite that same tone of blue—deep and hard in winter, luminous and silvery in summer—nor its reflection in the sea more sustained and, sometimes, in the trough of a wave, almost black; yet the term *Azur* is something more than a color: it is a transparency, the color of an intangible fluid illusion made of air, water and shadows. It is the color of a limpid gaze and the color of infinity, the color of the soul and of happy sun-drenched days.

Colette writing about the Riviera, had this to say: "Here there is a dominant blue which, though the color of dreams, also bathes all real things along the Provençal coast."

The Côte d'Azur—as Liégeard himself must have felt—is the Coast of Bliss. And it was precisely because most of those who have visited it have left behind them the memory of a love, or of countless joys, that the term came to be adopted in France and is now widely known in Europe and throughout the whole world. From everywhere, people started traveling to this privileged region. Berlioz described his stay there as "the best three weeks in my life". Théodore de Banville wrote: "One goes to Nice for a week and stays there for a whole lifetime". Poets and travelers have praised its delights—Stendhal in his *Mémoires,* and Nietzsche, who found there a "halcyon sky which shone for the first time in my life".

Countless writers as well as painters seem to have settled there at various times: from Alphonse Karr—who worked there as a gardener—to Colette and Prévert; from Picasso, who worked in ceramics during his stay, to Renoir, Signac, Léger, Chagall and many others, less famous perhaps, who went to the Riviera searching for a peaceful refuge.

All the courts of Europe were represented also; many a prince or sovereign, having been ousted from power, went there to conclude a destiny which, though lacking in glory, may have brought with it wisdom...

A host of testimony and memories have revealed a past whose picture is superimposed on the present. Of course, business and work go on there like anywhere else; but the place is pervaded by a carefree, hopeful mood.

From Toulon to Menton, the ancient trading posts of the Phenicians and the Greeks, the harbors into which Roman galleys once sailed, the creeks and hills from which lookouts scanned the horizon for Saracen raiders, the elegant resorts once frequented by 'royalty, the flower-bedecked cities of the *Belle Epoque* have now become distinctly cosmopolitan places where the living is very good indeed.

No other regions have thrived to quite the same extent as this in the past hundred years. Nice is now one of the main cities in France, and all along the coast numerous small towns have spread out their tentacles, while somehow managing to leave havens of peace for those seeking the quiet life and even solitude.

The Riviera is the only region in France where, on the same day, it is possible to go swimming in warm sea water and ski down the slopes of the high valleys—as if nature had wanted to make a bouquet of its beauties and good things!

JEAN VALBONNE

TOULON, THE HINGE OF AN ENTIRE REGION

By virtue of its location, enclosed inside its deeply indented bay and laid out on the slopes of the hills which protect it from the land side, Toulon is naturally something of a hinge for the entire region. The peninsulas which reach out protectively to the south are the extreme tip of French territory on the Mediterranean coast, between the Gulf of Lion in the west, and the Gulf of Genoa in the east. It also separates two regions and two aspects of the celebrated region of Provence.

On the one hand, the Provence of Mistral, with its coves, its white rocks and its landscape swept by the Mistral; on the other hand, from Hyères to Menton, the Riviera of flowers, red rocks, the enchantment of mild winters and dreamlike scenery.

Today we see Toulon as an ideal point of departure for touring the south of France. But in ancient times it was in the hands of warriors and navigators who were most attracted by the topography of its beautifully sheltered roadstead, a safe haven from which galleys, frigates and corvettes could set sail for eastern seas. The history of Toulon is largely military: over the centuries, Saracen raids and colonial expeditions made it essential for the city to fortify and arm

itself suitably—hence the rather grim, unpolished appearance of the port and its vicinity.

Historians say that Toulon was founded by Phenicians or Romans. After the triumph of the Barbarians, it was not until the time of Guillaume I, count of Provence that the city began to recover; but then the Moors came and ravaged the region. After its union with the French crown at the end of the 15th century, it had yet to undergo the invasion of the troops of Charles V. During the reign of Louis XIV the shipyards and port at last prospered, but a century later it was once more besieged. As the royalists had stirred up an insurrection in 1793, Toulon opened its port to the Anglo-Spanish fleet, whose officers were solemnly received at the town hall. This treachery aroused a storm of protest at the Convention. Bonaparte, then a mere captain, demonstrated his military genius during the siege. Having been threatened with total destruction, Toulon gradually emerged from its disgrace: during the colonial wars it recovered the full measure of its importance. The last dramatic action to take place there was the scuttling, in 1942, of the French Navy which was in danger of being taken over by the Nazis. For many years Toulon was known as the city of convicts, the mere sight of which horrified Stendhal when he visited the city. The sailors who thronged the steets were from all continents. Toulon was celebrated for its noisy nights and its dance halls.

The port district has lost none of its romantic flavor as a port of call, even though the city has changed appreciably in the meantime. Each evening, sailors out for a night on the town can be seen strolling around the narrow streets near the port.

Two views of Toulon: the port and inner harbor.

Nowadays one nas to go to the very heart of a city in order to form an opinion of it: all the outlying areas are very much alike, with tall cubic structures, parking lots and green areas where the trees have not yet had time to grow to any decent height. Toulon in no exception in this respect.

The Boulevard de Strasbourg marks the boundary of the old town, whose narrow streets are huddled between Place Puget,with its astonishing Trois-Dauphins fountain, shrouded in vegetation, and the Cours Lafayette, which is situated on the site of the old ramparts and where a most colorful market is held every morning. Further on is the Poissonerie, the fish market, with its tidal aromas, its fishermen and its fishwives who, in the midst of a lively sales-oriented cacophony, deftly handle the flashing silver shapes of hogfish, red mullet, moray and conger eels.

A stroll around Toulon will yield other delights: gardens with rare and aromatic plants

including cedars, magnolias and palm trees; museums of paintings, history and naval lore; and the old Tour Royale de la Mitre, which Louis XII originally built for the defense of the city and which was actually used for the most part as a prison! The passage of time, and styles, has left its mark in the cathedral of Sainte-Marie-Majeure.

The Rue d'Alger leads to the port. Much of the original decorative work in the port area has been destroyed; a notable survivor is Puget's famous set of cariatids, now on the façade of the Naval Museum, which stands on the site of the city hall which was destroyed by bombs. Like the arsenal, which is the center of this second-ranking naval port in France, the museum is open to visitors.

Left: street in old Toulon. Wrought-iron enclosure, the Admiralty. Above: Pier at the marina. Opposite: one of the famed cariatids masterfully sculpted by Puget, the Naval Museum.

Toulon should also be seen from the sea; this can be done by taking a boat trip around the harbor. It is also possible to drive out to the Saint-Mandrier peninsula, which closes the anchorage to the south, in order to get a superb view of the city and its backdrop of mountains.

Mount Faron is a remarkable belvedere overlooking the Toulon roadsteads as a whole.

There are plenty of interesting excursions which can be made from Toulon: in the direction of the port of La Seyne-sur-Mer, or Sanary Beach, beautifully decorated with tamarisk and palm trees, or towards the Ollioules Gorges and the abandoned village of Evenos; or northwards to Mount Caume and Solliès-Pont. Solliès-le-Vieux is perched on a granite outcrop. The total population of the village was no more than a hundred or so when it occurred to the poet Jean Aicard to stage one of his plays in order to attract visitors. His efforts were rewarded and new life was injected into the old village.

Battleships moored at Toulon. Above: one of the hills flanking the town. Lower left: Sanary Port. Below: view from Mount Faron.

HYÈRES TODAY AND YESTERDAY

Hyères is the most southerly of the Mediterranean resorts, and the one with the oldest reputation. As far back as the 18th century, the mildness of its winter climate astonished and delighted the privileged few who could enjoy it. During the 19th century the fame of this charming resort—also known as Hyères-les-Palmiers—spread across Europe as far as distant Russia, where the nobility shivered in their drafty palaces! In his book *Hyères, old and new,* M.-A. Denis gives an impressive list of the persons who stayed at Hyères: thirty sovereigns and princes, and hundreds of famous Frenchmen, Englishmen, Germans, Belgians, Spaniards, Italians and Romanians, and above all, Russians, including all the great families of St.Petersburg and Moscow. During his journey to France, Leo Tolstoy spent some time there in 1860, with his brother Nicholas, whom the climate was unable to save.

Hyères was once a port from which many Crusades set forth. Saint-Louis landed there on his way back from the Holy Land. A church was built in the 12th century, but stylistic changes in the 16th century adulterated its character to some extent. All around are old streets with picturesque names: Rue Barbacasse, Rue Paradis have retained their archaic appearance and include some valuable remnants from the distant past—in particular a skilfully restored 13th-century house.

The church of Saint-Louis, which is also 13th century, is associated with the memory of Saint Louis, king of France, who stopped to pray there.

Today the town is spreading, mainly along the coast, towards Hyères-Plage which is built up with beachfront villas and apartments as far as Port-Pothuau, a fishing harbor near the now disused Hyères salt works.

To the south, the coast is rather unusual for this part of France, being flat and swampy, while the Giens Peninsula is actually a former island linked to the mainland by two thin sandbanks

surrounding Pasquier Lagoon. The road runs along the waterfront to Giens, where the main sights are a ruined castle, a tower built under Richelieu and, in particular, a fine panoramic view of the Var coastline.

Left: palm-lined avenue in Hyères. Below: farming in Carqueranne. Above: view of one of the smaller ports along the Giens Peninsula. Below: view of the peninsula.

THE GOLDEN ISLES: PORQUEROLLES AND PORT-CROS

Situated opposite the jagged ridges of the Maures, which tower over the coastline, the Hyères Islands—Porquerolles, Port-Cros and Ile du Levant—provide the visitor with moments of idyllic seclusion and timeless beauty such as are rarely found nowadays. And yet these inlets and capes have their own history, involving Greeks, Romans and the monks of Lérins, who werè frequently attacked by pirates.

Francis I made the three islands into a marquisate, and decided to confer upon them the status of a territory of asylum, where criminals could enjoy impunity; this paradise promptly turned into a den of thugs and pirates who soon began to threaten the merchant ships from Toulon. Louis XIV restored order by driving these undesirable characters out. Forts, such as that of Sainte-Agathe, perched on a promontory on the island of Porquerolles, were built to repel the pirates.

In 1793, after the revolutionary army had retaken Toulon, the English and Spanish fleets dropped anchor off the islands. Bonaparte took the forts and their land. The last of the islands' military adventures took place: the landing of the Allies on 15 August. The military stayed for a long time on Port-Cros, which served as a target for the warships!

A decree was passed in 1963 making Port-Cros

a national nature and marine preserve. The island was thereby saved from the grasp of the real estate promoters and returned to nature; one of the island's landowners helped by donating 600 acres for this purpose. Port-Cros, which is more heavily wooded and steeper than Portquerolles, is a pearl of greenery on the azure sea. Its vegetation includes eucalyptus, pine, myrtle, lentisks, lavender and heather; it is moreover a bird sanctuary visited by flamingoes, wood-pigeons and cormorants. Work has started on the restoration of the old forts, and paths have been laid out. There is a small harbor, formerly a fishermen's village, opposite the small island of Bagau.

The island of Porquerolles, the biggest of the group, is also State-owned land and a fauna and flora preserve. Footpaths wind their way among the luxurious vegetation towards sandy beaches with a fringe of marine pines. The copses keep the air cool even in midsummer.

Levant Island, sheltered by some fairly sheer cliffs, is the domain of the nudists: its main community, appropriately named Heliopolis, the 'city of the sun', was founded in 1931.

Porquerolles. Left: road leading into the pine forest. View of the southern shore. Above: the fort and port of some years passing. Below: tiny island known as "Le Petit Langoustier" (The Little Lobsterer).

Upper left : seen above and below — the village, the port, and some of the wooly shoreline of Port-Cros Island. Lower left : the "main square", Porquerolles.

There are two roads which link the Hyères waterfront and the Gulf of Saint-Tropez—two attractive roads which illustrate the two aspects of this part of the Mediterranean coast. Route Nationale 98 crosses the massif through the Dom Forest, while RN 559 splits off before Bormes and stays close to the sea as far as La Croix-Valmer, at the entrance to the Saint-Tropez peninsula along the Maures Corniche.

Just after La Londe-des-Maures, RN 98 climbs to the Gratteloup Pass and then runs along several valleys between the slopes which are covered by the Dom Forest. To the north these slopes rise to 2,535 ft at La Sauvette, whereas the highest peaks nearer to the coast do not exceed 1,300 to 1,625 ft.

In the heart of the Maures Massif, which stretches northwards to the Argens Valley, there is a large forest and also a few villages. From west to east, they are: Pierrefeu, at the edge of a forest of the same name; Collobrières, in the midst of plantations of cork-oaks which supply a local industry; La Garde-Freinet, a former lair of the Saracens which has a Renaissance church, a Romanesque chapel and the ruins of a castle at La Croix-des-Maures. It is surrounded by a belt of chestnuts, pines and cork-oaks.

From Collobrières a winding road crosses the massif to Bormes-les-Mimosas, an old village with vaulted streets and posterns. It also has some very nice terraces with flower beds: those of the Place Gambetta and the castle of the Lords of Fos, which offers particularly superb views.

Bormes has now been greatly enlarged by the addition of a new town closer to the sea, and also a new port, the quays and building of which join the Corniche at Le Lavandou.

Bormes can also serve as a center for touring the interior of the massif, towards the chapel of

Notre-Dame de Constance, Pierre d'Avignon Point and the Dom Forest; the beautiful Corniche des Crêtes leads to Le Canadel.

This road runs for about twelve miles, past numerous small resorts well suited to family vacations and a complete rest. Between the two wars, Le Lavandou, which is sheltered by Cape Bénat and has a beach of fine sand and a picturesque harbor, was a favorite place of numerous artists and writers, who thrived on its tranquility and enjoyed the warmth of the local life. Since then tourism and real estate developments have turned this modest village into a lively resort, with summer vacationers and local fun-seekers!

The beaches stretch away to the east, towards Saint-Clair, Aiguebelle and Cavalière, where the shore is lined with sea-pines. There is a most pleasant footpath around Cape Nègre, not far from which ancient remains have been discovered.

Further to the east the road passes through Le Canadel and Le Rayol, whose villas are barely visible among the clusters of pines and banks of flowers along the slopes. The abundance of species, from rose-laurel to mimosa, makes a delightful sight in any season of the year. The beaches are well sheltered, nestling deep inside rocky inlets.

At the entrance to the bay between Cape Cavalaire and Cape Lardier is a more popular resort, Cavalaire; the French and American liberation forces landed on its superb beaches in August 1944.

Above: the shore road at Maures and Cape Nègre. Cavalaire beach. Left, opposite: an abandoned *mas*, or old homestead, in the Var Mountains near Babaou Pass. Right: 12th century church in Bormes-les-Mimosas.

THE TWO FACES OF SAINT-TROPEZ

Saint-Tropez has two faces: those of its past and present, its legend and its snobbishness—and ne'er the twain shall meet, as the saying goes. Visitors who appreciate the former should stay well away from the latter, and studiously avoid swelling the motley crowd which turns the waterfront, on summer days, into a hotter version of a fashionable Paris boulevard.

The deadline may be situated on the 15th of June, the date of the traditional festival of La Bravade, at which the crowd is more local in character. It celebrates both the Roman martyr, whose headless body washed ashore, and the victory of the inhabitants of Saint-Tropez over the Spanish galleys which, in 1637, laid siege to the waterfront. Having been ravaged too often by the Saracen pirates, the town was unable to recover its former activity. It did, however, preserve its charm—which in turn saved it by attracting large numbers of artists.

In 1892, Paul Signac had sailed from Roscoff on his boat "Olympia", intending to go around the world. He called at Saint-Tropez... and went no further! He kept his boat but bought a house and summoned his friends to the brightly colored little port: Maximilien Luce, Henri Cross, Camoin and then Bonnard, Vuillard, Marquet and Matisse responded to his appeal. They did so with the clear idea of assembling their works in a local museum. The marvelous Annonciade Museum, housed in an early 16th century chapel, imaginatively renovated for the purpose, thus came into being. This museum of Mediterranean painting, which was opened in 1955, contains works from the period of Divisionism and later, by Marquet, Matisse, Bonnard, Vuillard, Camoin, etc.

Saint-Tropez is also Colette, who, in her *La Treille Muscate*, tells of her love for the bay of Saint-Tropez. The book's title was also that of her house; she invited Dunoyer de Segonzac, another painter who was in love with this peninsula, to come and stay in her house to do the illustrations. Here is what she has to say in a passage from *La Naissance du Jour:* "La Treille Muscate, is this my last house ever? I gauge it and listen to it during the short inner night which immediately follows midday in these parts. The crickets and the new wattling which shelters the terrace both crackle, some insect or other crushes tiny embers between its wing-sheaths; the reddish bird in the pine calls out every ten seconds and the west wind,

Left and below: harbor and quay, St. Tropez. Village bell tower, place des Lices. Following pages: dusk, portside.

which hovers about my walls, does not ruffle the flat, dense, hard sea, whose rigid blue tones will become softer towards evening".

After the painters and novelists came the movie stars. Brigitte Bardot made her film *Et Dieu créa la femme*, which set her firmly on the road to glory, at Saint-Tropez, and then decided to settle there.

Saint-Trop', to give it its familiar name, has a dream-like image: the movements of brilliant colors beneath of walls, the water lapping against the quays, white sails dancing in the sun...

With its gulf and peninsula, it is a microcosm of the charms of the Riviera as a whole, and its

various sights and pleasures. A delightful miniature Venice was built only a few decades ago on a previously unoccupied part of the deeply indented bay; like those of the City of the Doges, its inhabitants can step right of their doors into boats. The houses are painted, and there are small playgrounds for children which are quiet in winter but noisy in summer. The light is reflected from the water onto the bridges across the canals... From La Foux to Saint-Tropez the road runs along the sea front, past villas which look out over the bay.

Just inland are two old villages: Grimaud and Cogolin. Grimaud is well endowed, having the ruins of a feudal castle, arcaded houses, a

Romanesque church and a Templars' House! It is thought that the village was the Athenapolis of the ancient Greeks, where the beautiful Phryne, the model-cum-mistress of Praxiteles, was once exiled. Clearly the nudity which is so dear to Saint-Tropez has truly ancient origins!

Cogolin cannot quite match this,but its Romanesque church, its clock tower and its nettle-trees, beneath the old ramparts, make a charming picture. It also has its own marina, with terraced waterfront.

The peninsula consists of a series of rocky headlands sheltering beaches of light colored sand. The secluded privacy of this landscape is somewhat troubled by the crowds of vacationers in the summer months. Gassin is strategically situated, behind its ramparts, on higher ground— the easier to spot Saracen raiders approaching from the sea. The highest point of the peninsula is Les Moulins de Paillas (The Windmills of Paillas), now in ruins.

Closer to the coast and to Cape Camarat, Ramatuelle has grown towards the sea, but the old village, laid out on the slopes in the midst of vineyards, has not lost its character. The actor Gérard Philippe (1922-1959) lies buried in the graveyard near the village.

When the fine weather comes, the beaches near Saint-Tropez, Tahiti Beach and the Pampelonne Bight are quite crowded with sun-worshippers. It is, however, still possible to find in the peninsula isolated footpaths and out-of-the-way corners where nature still reigns supreme.

Left: the old village of Grimaud and a view of Grimaud Port. Right: typical Ramatuelle house, chapel erected in honour of Gerard Philipe, actor and frequent sojourner in the village.

FROM SAINTE-MAXIME
TO SAINT-RAPHAËL

On the north shore of Saint-Tropez Bay, Sainte-Maxime is quite a recent resort, which marks the beginning of a series of highly popular beaches.

The one closest to Sainte-Maxime is La Martelle. Behind it are the wooded hills of the Maures Massif, which have not been spared by forest fires. Beyond La Nartelle are Le Val-d'Esquières and Les Issambres, in both of which real estate development has taken place a little too rapidly. Lastly comes Saint-Aygulf, with a rocky shore, and pine and eucalyptus groves.

The entire coast consists of magnificent sandy beaches, but the coast road runs very close to the sea—with the heavy summer traffic that that involves. After the mouth of the Argens we come to Fréjus and Saint-Raphaël, which have now met in one large built-up area.

The seaside resort of Saint-Raphaël originally became fashionable because of a writer—professionally a journalist and pamphleteer, but temperamentally a poet—who really put it on the map. As early as Roman times, however, Saint-Raphaël was already a vacation center much esteemed by the aristocracy. The present Casino is built on the site of palaces and thermal baths.

In the second half of the 19th century, Alphonse Karr, who had already abandoned Paris and literature for Nice and the cultivation of flowers, discovered this tranquil haven while sailing along the coast. He stayed for a week and found the place so delightful that he decided to settle there. He was to spend the last fifteen years of his life in Saint-Raphaël, where he died in the midst of his flowers. Lamartine dedicating a letter-poem to him, praising the wisdom of a writer who had preferred the spade to the pen and the scent of roses to the incense of glory!

Since the war Saint-Raphaël has greatly developed its facilities, its harbor and its beaches. It has a center for seawater therapy, at the Marine Institute, and a Museum of Underwater Archeology. The beaches are safe and the town is almost entirely modern, even its church in the Byzantine style. All that remains of the old village is the 12th century Templars' Church. Its watchtower testifies to the role it once played as a fortress during the time of the Saracen raids along the coast!

Ports of St. Maxime, St. Raphaël, and, below, St. Aygulf.

FRÉJUS, ROMAN AND ROMANESQUE

Fréjus is a Roman creation. The impressive remains which can still be seen there today are proof of the importance assumed over the centuries by the way station which Caesar established in 49 BC. In those days the Phoceans of Marseille had already set up a colony on the site, but it was the Roman emperor who gave the port its prosperity and the city its name: *Forum Julium* or *Julii*, the market of Julius.

The sea used to come right up to the city walls which were later built by Augustus. The 200 galleys captured at the battle of Actium were sent to Forum Julii, while the veterans of the 8th Legion settled there with their families. A great deal of construction was soon undertaken: a lighthouse, a pantheon, the amphitheater and the aqueduct, the ruins of which are still visible. The waters of the Siagne were channeled from 25 miles away to supply the city. Very soon the city and its port grew very considerably. The port,

which covered an area of 55 acres, had a mile and a half of wharves and led to the sea along a 500-yard canal. Its entrance was marked by two large towers; one of them, which was altered in the Middle Ages, still exists near Fréjus and enables one to form an idea of the location of the docks.

The *Pax Romana*, by denying Forum Julii its military activity, marked the beginning of its decline. The navy was phased out towards the end of the 2nd century, while the inhabitants increasingly sank into a life of ease and indulgence.

The decadence of Rome naturally led to that of the city. The sea encroached on the land, while the invasions of Saracens and pirates left the monuments in ruins. By the 10th century there was little left of the colony but rubble. Seaborne silt clogged up the port and led to the formation of a huge swampy plain. It was filled in during the Revolution to avoid malaria. In the 12th century, however, Christianity began to take up where Rome had left off: the cathedral was built on the site of a temple to Jupiter; a Romanesque cloister surrounding an old well was built next to the baptistry, which is thought to have been founded late in the 4th century.

These structures, together with the Bishops'

Palace and the Roman ruins, account for the exceptional archeological value of Fréjus. Some of the town is new, having been rebuilt after the disaster of the Malpasset Dam in 1959, which caused more than 400 deaths and partly destroyed the town. Only the ancient monuments withstood the torrential floodwaters. The amphitheater, the classical theater and the remains of the aqueduct convey a picture of Roman life in the early years of the Christian era.

Fréjus: view of famous Roman ruins. Leaf of cathedral door (XVIth c.). Triptych (same period).

DRAGUIGNAN AND THE VAR HINTER-LAND

A huge forest stretches up behind Fréjus to higher ground in the east, where it joins the Tanneron Massif. In the middle, Bagnols-en-Forêt is a village perched on top of a hill from which one can visit the Blavet Gorges.

To the south of this area, road and rail lead to Le Muy, Les Arcs and Draguignan which at one time was the *Préfecture* of Var. It is an important market town which has preserved its Provençal character, including shaded square and fountains. Its name derives from *Dragonia,* in connection with the 5th century legend of the dragon which is supposed to have terrorized those parts. Saint Hermentarius, later bishop of Antipolis, had come to evangelize the region, founding a monastery related to the abbey of Lérins. The inhabitants were living in constant fear of a fabulous monster which laid waste their farms and croplands. Hermentarius boldly strode out in front of the beast and rammed his bishop's staff down its throat, thus delivering the city and, incidentally, winning souls for the Church.

Ever since then a festival has taken place every Whit Monday at the monastery of Saint-Hermentaire. It was to commemorate this exploit that the town took the name of Draguignan, with a coat-of-arms described thus: "Silver dragon on field of gules".

Over the centuries the community grew considerably. Ramparts were built in order to

cloister and conventual buildings. Having been sold in 1793 and later undergone renovations which were not in the best of taste, it was bought by the State in 1854 and restored to its original appearance.

There are other interesting places north of

Draguignan: Callas, with its picturesque narrow streets; Bargemon and its medieval remains; Seillans; Fayence, which has a wrought-iron belltower; Callian, huddled around its castle, high up on a rocky spur; and lastly Montauroux, on the road to Grasse.

protect the inhabitants, the vassals of the counts of Provence, from the barbarian raiders. But the wars of religion brought new troubles. In 1559 Antoine de Richieu, lord of Mauvans, who was on his way to Draguignan to negotiate with the Catholics, was lynched by the mob and his remains were tossed to the dogs or down the gutters! This event marked the beginning of many years of turmoil.

Toulon's fall from favor after its treachery in 1793 had the effect of promoting Draguignan to the status of county town, or *chef-lieu,* and then chief town of the *département.* Its loss of that status, a few years ago, generated much ill-feeling.

Past Lorgues, an old village in the midst of pines and vineyards, is Thoronet Abbey, founded by the Cistercians in Provence during the 12th century. Its style is a mixture of Gothic and Romanesque: its structures include a church, a

Above: the tiny City of Arcs. Below: view of Draguignan. Right, opposite: road winding through the countryside outside Fayence. Village house standing out amidst the plain.

28

FROM THE TANNERON TO THE ESTEREL

From Fréjus to La Napoule Bay, RN 7 and, slightly further north, the remarkable Esterel expressway cut across two mountain ranges which are both charming and grandiose: the Tanneron in the north, and Esterel in the south.

The first of these, which is less well known than the second, consists of a number of hills whose altitude barely exceeds 1,600 ft. As in the case of the Esterel, however, here also the hills are often steep enough to look like mountains. They are heavily wooded, with few roads, and are divided by inaccessible valleys. On the north slopes, particularly from Tanneron to Mandelieu and Auribeau to Pégomas this landscape is alive with the brilliant color of the mimosa from January to March. The roads in this area, particularly from Tanneron to Pégomas, are a delight as they pass between hillsides literally carpeted with richly scented wild and cultivated vegetation. Traces of the terrible fire which swept through this region in 1969 and cost the lives of the Gray family, have virtually disappeared. The beauty of the mimosa is clearly matched only by its vitality!

Beyond the village of Le Tanneron, the road winds its way down the side of wooded slopes towards the large man-made lake of Saint-Cassien, a beautiful place for water sports.

The Auberge des Adrets, on the other side of the expressway going south, dates from the 17th century. The famous bandit Gaspard de Besse took refuge there. The Pas de l'Esterel leads into another massif, with vegetation quite unlike that to be found on Le Tanneron. However it also has valleys between mountain peaks: Mount Vinaigre (2,000 ft.), the Pic de l'Ours, the Pic de l'Aurelle and the Pic du Cap Roux, and outcroppings of red prophyry carpeted with pines and cork oaks.

There are a number of rather difficult roads across this massif; it is, for that reason, still wild and unspoilt. At the bottom of a ravine, the stream known as the Grenouillet winds along into the Mal-Infernet, a defile more than a mile long. The crystal-clear water runs over the pebbles, while pines cling to the rock faces far above, with narcissuses and violets growing at their feet. The stones are covered with cistuses and lentisks. Everywhere one turns one finds a riot of color: green pines, the azure sky, sheer red rock faces dropping away towards the blue waters of the Mediterranean...

Left: rock formations in the Esterel area. Below: holiday resort in the awesome setting of the Tanneron.

THE GOLDEN CORNICHE

This may well be the most beautiful part of the Mediterranean coastline of France! The contours of the terrain are fuller, and less abrupt than beyond Nice, both landscape and vegetation are exceedingly varied and, above all else, the colors in this area reach their highest intensity.

Beyond Saint-Raphaël the coast is fairly flat until the Tour du Dramont which overlooks the small roadstead of Agay, at the foot of the Rastel (935 ft.) the most westerly peak of the Esterel Massif. Dramont beach was the scene, on the 15th August 1944, of the Allied landing in Provence. A stele commemorates the event. Roman amphoras more than 2,000 years old have been discovered just offshore.

From Anthéor onwards the beaches begin to yield to rocky cliffs, buttresses of the Pic du Cap Roux, whose slopes tower over the whole of the Golden Corniche. The road, which is situated halfway up the slope, was built on the initiative of Abel Ballif, the first president of the Touring-Club de France, en 1903. Each turn in the road provides the traveler with new views of the capes and inlets which stretch away towards La Napoule—a scene which, with the changing light at various times of the day, acquires a range of magic qualities.

The villas of Le Trayas lie buried in the vegetation, including mimosas and succulent plants of the hillside. In the 17th century the small port of Figuerette was a tuna fishing center, using large nets which were left in position for months at a time. Today it is a harbor for pleasure craft, well sheltered from the wind. The Esterel Massif is an effective barrier against the onslaught of the Mistral, which spends its fury on the upland ridges and, beyond the Corniche, is quite mild.

There are some trails below the road, and a number of paths leading down to small inlets, not all of which have been subjugated by the intrusion of private residences.

From Esquillon Point—the scene of a diversionary landing in 1944—there is a fine view along the coast from Cap Roux to Cap d'Antibes. Théoule, at the foot of the mountain, is a delightful little harbor with a beach, just off the road, where it is possible, out of season, to recover some of the primeval tranquility of this area!

At the outlet of the Maure Vieil Valley, which contains a nature reserve, another yacht harbor has been built: La Rague. Napoule Bay widens towards Cap Croisette and the Lérins Islands. In La Napoule, with its castle restored by the American artist Henry Clews, its recent marina and its beaches, one really feels that one is almost in Cannes, with its crowds and assorted delights...

Upper right: Théoule. Below: distinctive hues of the rock face at Esterel. Above: boats at La Rague yacht harbor.

CANNES AND THE BAY

Cannes is the most recent and perhaps also the most attractive of the big resorts along the coast.

At the beginning of the last century all that stood between the slopes of Le Suquet and La Croisette Point was a humble fishing village, with a monastery on slightly higher ground. Today a sumptuous town spreads out like a fan around the superb bay, which is protected from the wrath of the sea by the Lérin Islands and festooned by the undulating contours of the amethyst or opal Esterel Massif.

Cannes owes its good fortune to the excellence of its position, its beaches of fine sand, and the succession of plateaux which stretch up as far as the Pre-Alps, protecting it from the cold north winds and allowing the most luxurious vegetation to grow on its terraces.

It is also indebted to its industrious inhabitants and far-sighted leaders who proved able to attract well-endowed foreigners and open up this privileged haven to those who were able to make and unmake reputations.

In the 19th century, Cannes quickly outpaced its rivals as a gathering place for the elegant. Gentlemen and ladies of rank and substance rode along the Boulevard de l'Impératrice, now La Croisette, either on horseback or in luxurious carriages. Men of letters and queens of the theater used to meet there to exchange the latest gossip.

Then after the First World War came the *Belle Epoque*, as it was called—the period which was so well described by Michel-Georges-Michel, an acute observer of the social scene, in his book *La Nouvelle Riviéra*. Most of European high society and a great many exiled—or merely visiting—monarchs used to meet there on the best of terms, from the king of Sweden to the king of Portugal, not to mention the shah of Persia and a host of Russian *kniasi*.

The riotous beauties of Parisian society formed the retinue of kings with whom they engaged in night-long revelries, while studiously creating scandals which provided material for the press back home. While the chroniclers were kept busy, the artists were also there in force, to record the ephemeral elegance of the fashions of the day. Van Dongen (1877-1968) known as a "tamed" member of the Fauvist movement, was there showing the way to the noted portrait painter Jean-Gabriel Domergue (1889-1962).

Cannes has moved with the times. Nowadays it is in full view of the whole world; for a brilliant fortnight once a year it is the capital of world cinema. The stars charm their royal highnesses and sometimes, as in the case of Grace of Monaco —marry them!

Any kings that are still to be found in Cannes are the kings of American commercial empires or of Middle Eastern oilfields, whose glittering yachts can be seen swaying gently in Canto Harbor.

Before the Roman conquest there was a hamlet named Oxybia at the foot of the hill on which the old town of Le Suquet is situated. It was destroyed by the invaders. A century later in 69 AD, the troops of Othon and Vitellius fought a bloody battle which ended to the advantage of the barbarians. However, they withdrew, and the

Cannes. Left: two glimpses of the Old Port. Right: hill and Suquet church—steps, palms in the original village that eventually became a major resort. Following page: summertime on the beach at La Croisette's grand hotel front.

Romans built a castle to defend the coast and the *Via Aurelia*.

When the abbots of Lérins, who had settled on Saint-Honorat Island, managed to acquire this part of the coast, they quickly built a tower on the rock, so that lookouts could more easily spot the approaching sails of Saracen warships and sound the alarm.

The name of Cannes apparently derives from Cannis or Canoïs, meaning "port of canes or reeds". In the Middle Ages the port was merely a fishing hamlet among the bamboo thickets which grew in such abundance on the banks of the Siagne.

Cannes began its rise to fame and fortune with a chance visit from a rich winter visitor. In 1834, Lord Brougham, the Lord High Chancellor of England, was on his way to Nice for his customary winter vacation, and had just reached the Var bridge which in those days marked the boundary of the kingdom of Sardinia, when his coachman informed him that the road was closed. As there was an epidemic of cholera in Provence, the Sardinian authorities were relentlessly turning back all travelers. He therefore had to go back along the Antibes road looking for somewhere to stay. There was a modest inn at Cannes. Lord Brougham was instantly taken with the charm of the coast at this point and decided to make it his winter residence. The man who was once described as "one of the most ruthless cannibals of modern times", on account of his extremely harsh treatment of the workers, invited a steady stream of rich Englishmen to Cannes. By the time of his death in 1868, at the age of 89, Cannes had already come to rival Nice.

George Sand was invited there by another literary lady, Juliette Adam, whose property at Les Bruyères was a meeting place for distinguished guests. The tragic actress Rachel died at Le Cannet. And Prosper Mérimée, a faithful winter visitor, wrote to his friends: "Not a cloud in the sky, no wind, a magnificent sun. I am eating peas, and there are ripe strawberries to be had in the woods. Cannes is the land of milk and honey."

His words are still true today: Cannes still draws the world's millionnaires to its palatial hotels and its casinos. Yet snobbery and elegance have not killed off the place's local color or everyday life. While rich winter visitors drive nonchalantly along the Croisette in their Rolls-Royces, pensioners play pétanque on the waterfront and the housewives chat from window to window in the narrow streets of Le Suquet. From the terrace there is a sweeping view of the whole town the roadstead and the islands. La Castre museum, at the foot of the medieval tower, contains Mediterranean exhibits from ancient times and *objets d'art* from all over the world.

Cannes. La Croisette the Hotel Carlton. Right: Port-Canto and la Napoule.

ISLANDS OF LEGEND

From Croisette Point to La Napoule there is a succession of beaches and pleasure harbors. From January onwards the hills of Super-Cannes and the Corniche du Paradis, behind the town, are lit up with the brilliance of mimosas in bloom. In the distance, the Lérins Islands lie indolently on the mother-of-pearl smoothness of the sea.

The larger of the two islands, Sainte-Marguerite, which is two miles long, is closer to the mainland; for the most part it is covered with pines and eucalyptus trees. However, it was to the second island that Saint Honorat withdrew in the 4th century. His retreat was discovered fairly quickly, and disciples flocked there to join him and to found a monastery. As the island was out of bounds to women, Marguerite, the sister of Honorat, founded a religious community for women on the neighboring island—hence its present name. Yet the holy man granted his sister only one visit a year, "during the season when the almond trees are in flower". Marguerite promptly planted an almond tree and prayed so hard for a chance to see her brother more often that the almond tree began to bloom every month! Seeing in this miracle a sign of the divine intention, Honorat allowed Marguerite to come as often as she liked.

The fortress, which is also named after the saint, was built by Richelieu and enlarged by Vauban, the famous military architect of the 17th century. For many years it was a State prison. Its most illustrious inmate was the Man in the Iron Mask, whom historians have successively identified as the adulterine brother of Louis XIV, an accomplice of the notorious poisoner Marie-Madeleine de Brinvilliers and a doctor of Louis XIII. Another famous prisoner was Marshal Bazaine, who was accused of treason after the defeat of Napoleon III at Sedan, and who was imprisoned on the island in 1874. He escaped eight months later, though it is unlikely that he did so in the daring manner described to tourists (down the cliffs on a rope); instead, he is thought to have slipped out disguised as a peasant woman, by the skilful use of inside help.

The fortress of Sainte-Marguerite, which has been restored for some years, is a youth center where ballet and concerts are performed each season.

For a short while after the dissolution of the monastic orders at the Revolution, Saint-Honorat Island was the property of a former actress at the Théâtre-Français, who lived there for twenty years. There is no way of knowing whether she did so for the sake of solitude, or in order to hide some secret love. In 1859 the monastery was restored to religious use, and ten years later the Cistercian monks of Sénanque settled there. The dignified keep was built in the 15th century. Parts of the cloister are from the 7th century, while the vaults are from the 10th. There are a number of chapels on the island, as well as two ovens for heating cannon balls, built on the orders of Napoleon in 1794. The cemetery of French soldiers killed in the Crimean campaign in 1855, on Sainte-Marguerite, makes a moving sight.

Pine trees and rocky terrain of St. Honorat Island. Right: two views of St. Marguerite Fort—the cloisters and the convent church.

GRASSE, AN AMPHITHEATER OVERLOOKING THE SEA

Basking in the southern sun, in a setting of azure hills, Grasse is the city of perfumes. The carnations from the hothouses of Nice and Antibes, the mimosas on the hillsides at Tanneron and the fields of jasmines of neighboring communities provide essences for the modern factories which have replaced the workshops of the past. In the Grasse region there are about twenty such facilities which receive their raw materials not only from Provence but also from the whole of France, and even from abroad in the case of certain rare essences or products such as grey amber, a minute quantity of which is sufficient to "fix" the perfume.

It is possible to visit the perfume factories of Grasse, which are, in a sense, laboratories where the alchemists of modern times devise subtle blends whose composition and effects are a closely guarded secret. The fragrance of a perfume is judged just like the *bouquet* of a wine.

This industry is closely linked to the history of Grasse, where it was preceded by leather tanning; in fact one led naturally to the other, when perfumed gloves came into fashion in the 16th century. In the manner of the Italian republics, Grasse, which had been founded by Rodoard, the governor of the countship of Antibes, had conducted its own administration as a free city and prospered by business—until the count of Provence laid hands on it. For centuries afterwards the beautiful city was ravaged by invasions, pirate raids and epidemics. After it had become attached to France, Grasse still had to undergo the depredations of the armies of Charles V, and those of the duke of Savoy. Even so, it continued to develop until the Revolution, as can be seen from the fine residences which can still be seen today: the Maison Isnard and the Château Clapiers-Cabris, now the Fragonard Museum.

The brilliant and somewhat frivolous life of this painter of the graces of the 18th century is a mirror image of the kind of lives led by the city's rich families. The Revolution passed away, and then came the Empire. In 1807 the attractive Pauline Bonaparte, being estranged from her husband Prince Borghese of Rome, and having quarreled with her brother the emperor, took refuge in Grasse, seeking peace and quiet. Every afternoon, the beautiful princess was carried in her sedan to the shade of the holm-oaks—in what is now known as Princess Pauline's Garden.

With both climate and exposure distinctly in its favor, Grasse then became a resort of some note, in which Queen Victoria used to spend her winters. A number of grand hotels were built along the esplanade of the terrace overlooking the old town, which is particularly worth a visit. Steep narrow streets and stairs lead down to its old market-places and houses, its Notre-Dame cathedral, which has a fine 18th-century twin staircase at the entrance, as well as its museums which contain some priceless collections of furniture, *objets d'art* and luxury items, documents, and old tools—all of which tell us so much about life under the *ancien régime,* both in high society and on the farm.

Grasse. Left: arcades along the Place aux Aires, the covered market, the entrance to the Hotel de Cabris, the rue de l'Evêché, and the Sarrazin Tower. Same page: view of the original city from the Gardens and la Fontette lane.

NEAR GRASSE:

Grasse has grown along the side of the mountain, eastwards towards Nice through Magagnosc and Châteauneuf-de-Grasse, and westwards towards Peymeinade, on the plain, and Cabris, which is built on a spur. The terrace on which the 17th-century church is situated towers almost vertically over the valley, and provides one with a superb view of the Tanneron Massif, and beyond that the Mediterranean and the Lérins Islands.

A road winds its way down through the olive groves towards Spéracédès and Saint-Cézaire, which is famous for the stalactites and stalagmites of its caves. Their strange shapes have given rise to the names of the various underground chambers: the Hall of Draperies, the Organs, the Fairies' Alcove, etc. Beyond them is an impressive chasm. The village is situated at the edge of a plateau which drops away abruptly towards the Siagne Gorges. The view from behind the village is breathtaking. Another road runs along the gorges, climbing to Mons, at 2,600 ft., another typically picturesque hamlet. The backroads of this region are most rewarding, and are not heavily traveled, even in the high season. The road from Mons to Seillans lies near the prohibited area of the Canjuers army camp. The desert panoramas are strongly reminiscent of the Far West!

North of Grasse, the Plateau Napoléon marks the place where Napoléon, on his return from the island of Elba, halted briefly before moving off along the road—then a mere path—which now bears his name. The Route Napoléon climbs quickly above Grasse and reaches the plateau of Saint-Vallier, with ample views of the coastline. Saint-Vallier, at 2,440 ft., has a very healthy climate, while its abundant vegetation contrasts nicely with the arid landscape which lies a little further on. Built in a daring corniche style, the road swings around in a huge loop past Pas de Faye and the Nans Valley, reaching 3,250 ft. at Escragnolles, and staying at that altitude south of Mount Audibergue, which is the closest ski resort to Grasse and Cannes. A chairlift runs to the top of the mountain at 5,340 ft.; the view along the coast at this point is splendid.

The villages of Andon and Caille can be reached from Séranon, on the Route Napoléon. A huge plateau extends around the Doire and the Logis-de-Pin, cutting across the Artuby Torrent, at the junction of two other roads. One of these runs south down to Comps, which leads to the unspoilt Artuby Gorges, while the other, to the north, runs along the plateau as far as La Foux and Saint-Auban. The Saint-Auban Rift, beyond the ridge on which the village stands, is a gigantic gash in the mountain which forms a little-known gorge.

After the Logis-de-Pin, the Route Napoléon reaches the Luens Pass (3,575 ft.) and the hamlet of La Garde, soon after which Castellane and its Virgin's Rock come into view. This is the gateway to the Verdon Gorges and the Alps.

Left: an old gateway in Grasse. Below: Saint-Cézaire and outside St. Vallier. Above: view of Cabris. Forest road on the outskirts of town. Samples of local artisanry.

FROM VALLAURIS TO JUAN-LES-PINS

By crossing the hills to the east of Cannes one can reach the Saint-Antoine Pass, which leads to Vallauris. From here there is a fine view of the whole of Cannes Bay, and, in the other direction, of Vallauris, the Nice area and the distant snow-capped peaks of the frontier range.

Ceramics are to Vallauris what perfume is to Grasse. Its association with this craft began four hundred years ago; Picasso, who lived there for several years, discovered an art form which he quickly mastered. There are many ceramists and potters along the coast, but at Vallauris their work amounts to a real industry. The quality varies, of course, but the number of dedicated artists endowed with good taste is still high.

Antibes is where most of Picasso's ceramic work is to be seen. He is, however, represented at Vallauris with a bronze *Man with sheep* which he presented to the town and which adorns the small square outside the Italianate church. The Roma-nesque chapel of the castle also contains a work by the same painter, *War and peace,* an enormous composition on wood, which covers the vault and walls of the chapel. The other rooms in the museum house collections of older ceramics and paintings.

The town's appearance has been altered by the prevalence of architectural cubism in the outlying areas. A road links it to Golfe-Juan, where the road begins to run along parallel to the sea, past beaches and restaurants, as far as Juan-les-Pins.

Golfe-Juan was where Napoléon I landed on 1 March 1815, on his way back from Elba. Antibes, however, refused to rally to his support, and the emissaries sent by the ex-emperor were taken prisoner. Napoléon then turned towards Cannes, where the welcome was quite as chilly. After that he set out towards the Alps. It was not until Lyon that he began to feel his venture stood some chance of success.

Juan-les-Pins was only a suburb of Antibes at the beginning of the century. Now it is a town of 50,000 inhabitants. An American millionaire, Frank J. Gould, set it on the road to fame and fortune by building a casino and a large hotel: during the *Belle Epoque* Juan was certainly a very

popular resort among the moneyed classes. After the war it continued to be a favorite meeting-place for celebrities and movie stars and consolidated the status of the French Riviera as *the* place to go in the summer. More particularly during the past twenty years Juan-les-Pins has become more democratic: the beaches and the cafés are now crowded with a broader cross-section of society in summer. At night, scenes of similar animation take place in the numerous cabarets and night-clubs in the area.

Vallauris. Picasso's famed *Man with sheep* on the square of the tiny area marking the original city; samples of some of his much acclaimed ceramic work. Above and right: Golfe-Juan port and beach. Singular Esterel coastline at the Bay of Cannes.

ANCIENT ANTIBES: RAMPARTS AND FLOWERS

The town of Antibes—the Antipolis of antiquity—is thought to have been founded in the 4th century BC by the Greeks of Massilia. The name of this early trading post and port of call—"opposite the city"—derives from its location, across the water from Nice.

When the Romans supplanted the Greeks, the city became Latinum Antipolis; several authors mention it as an important place in the region. A theater, arsenal and aqueduct were built, while sailors and fishermen settled along the shore. The barbarian invasions destroyed this prosperity, and until the early 4th century AD, when the first market was established, Antibes was something of a ghost town. The union of Provence and France made it a frontier post with the States of Savoy. Francis I and then Henry IV had both built fortified enclosures. The town's new status required an extension of its defenses, and Vauban completed these by building the famous Fort Carré, whose massive hulk still towers over the waterfront, and the ramparts facing out to sea.

The memory of Bonaparte is associated with Antibes. In 1794 he was in charge of the defense of the coast; he moved his family, which he was supporting himself, into a modest house. Madame Laetitia went to wash her laundry in the stream, while the young sisters, who were one day to be princesses, roamed the countryside picking fruit from neighboring orchards as they went. When Robespierre fell, a number of people suspected that the revolutionary general had had something to do with it. He was briefly imprisoned in the Fort Carré which he had been instructed to defend!

The setting of Antibes is generally unchanged, apart from the large marina which has replaced the old harbor. The town has steadily grown in all

directions, in the midst of the orchards and fields of flowers which have played such a part in its wealth. Carnations and anemones are the main products, being grown in hothouses covering millions of square yards. There are also many nurseries, which supply all the gardens of the Riviera with shrubs and succulent plants.

The narrow streets of the old town, a short way behind the sea-front ramparts, are situated at the foot of the Château Grimaldi (14th-16th centuries), the square tower of which looks down over the city. Some of its rooms contain exhibits of Gallo-Roman archeology and modern paintings; some others were made available to Picasso in 1946. He left the museum those works which he had created in the château and enriched it with a great deal of pottery, sculpture and tapestry of the period, thus making it a remarkable Picasso museum. The Bastion Saint-André, at the end of the ramparts, contains finds made during underwater explorations in the cove of St-Roch, including amphoras, inscriptions and assorted wreckage from Greek and Etruscan galleys.

Antibes. From left to right: Fort Carré, the inner courtyard, the gardens near the ramparts, the castle. Above: the Old Town and the city ramparts. Lower left: the castle terrasse, now the Picasso Museum.

CAP D'ANTIBES

This long, hilly promontory, which is well covered with woods, is a familiar outline on the Mediterranean horizon. A road runs around and into the interior of the cape, providing beautiful views of the coast and mountains, virtually throughout its entire length. The slopes of the hill are covered with sumptuous properties, right up to the plateau of La Garoupe, where one is treated, on clear days, to a panorama ranging from Saint-Tropez all the way to Bordighera, in Italy.

The 12th-century chapel of Notre Dame has two naves connected by broad arcades, and contains some strange votive offerings, as well as a 14th-century icon brought back from Sebastopol after the Crimean campaign, a black silk from the same source, and a 16th-century painted panel attributed to Louis Bréa.

Our Lady of La Garde, the patron of Antibes, is venerated in one of the naves: Our Lady of Beauty, the patron of artists and gardens, is to be found in another nave. Lastly, Our Lady of the Safe Haven, the patron of seafarers, is carried each year from La Garoupe to Antibes and back in a procession of sailors and fishermen. This pilgrimage takes place on the first Sunday of July.

The Antibes lighthouse, which was rebuilt after the Germans had destroyed its predecessor in 1944, is also situated at La Garoupe. It is visible to ships at ranges of 40 to 50 miles and to aircraft at between 155 and 185 miles. It is one of the most powerful on the Riviera. From all points along the coast, as the evening sky turns a shade of light lilac, from La Croisette to the Baie des Anges, from all the terraces of the hinterland between Magagnosc and Vence, its regular pulse of light cuts fleetingly across the sky.

Around the cape, the gardens of sumptuous hotels and luxury villas run right down to the

small rocky creeks which form its coastline. The mountain terraces of the hinterland do not, strictly speaking, end at the shore: they extend downwards, through the transparent bluish water, past madrepores and schools of rockfish.

The Cape of Antibes and view of the coast crested by mountains. Also seen from the mountains. Above: a glimpse of La Garoupe Chapel's, bell in a wel-known spot on the Cape amongst the pines.

FROM THE VILLAGES OF THE PAST
TO THE CITY OF THE FUTURE

The hinterland between Cannes and Cagnes, beyond the autoroute, forming a triangle with the roads from Grasse to Cannes and Grasse to Nice, is a hilly region clad in groves of pine and olive trees. Each ridge carries a village, and each vale shelters a stream: the Valmasque, the Brague and the Mardaric. Winding roads climb from the depths of the gorges, up the wooded slopes, from one hamlet to the next. Here the Provençal character of the villages is more pronounced than in the Grasse area: Mougins, with its jasmine, Valbonne with its grapes and Biot with its pottery.

Mougins, which is admirably situated on an isolated peak, towers over the surrounding landscape, from the sea to the Gorges du Loup. This former fief of Lérins Abbey contains the remains of some ramparts, a fortified gate and a 15th-century church whose belltower is a belvedere. The land slopes away to the Val de Mougins, on the Grasse road, and also towards Notre-Dame-de-Vie, which was once a center for pilgrimage. Picasso spent his final years at Notre-Dame-de-Vie, and died there in 1973.

Then, passing between the private village of Castellanas and the plateau of Peyniblou, the road proceeds to Valbonne, whose origins can be traced back to the foundation in 1199 of an abbey of the Chalais order. The village then came under Lérins. Its present appearance is that which it was given by Augustin de Grimaldi in the 16th century: that of a chessboard, with streets intersecting each other at right angles. Its shaded central square, consisting of thirteen arcades, dates from the time of Louis XIV. Villas have been built around it, but the characteristic narrow streets in the heart of the village, their houses decorated with flowers, still remain. Every winter, the Grape Festival, with floats and majorettes, is held in honor of the *servan,* a golden table grape, preserved by means of a special local process, which can be consumed until April.

Further north, one comes to the sanctuary of Notre-Dame de Brusc and the village of Opio, which has a 14th-century oil mill and jasmine fields used to supply the perfume industry. A succession of pine groves and olive trees stretches from Valbonne to Biot, where we find another arcaded square, two fine altarpieces by Bréa of the Nice school in the church, and a tradition of pottery which was at its height in the 17th century when the village boasted almost 40 small factories. In those days jars were hand-molded and baked in a kiln at 800 degrees Centigrade. A number of potteries remain, as well as a renowned glassworks, where it is possible to see glass being blown by hand. The Fernand Léger Museum, on the road to Antibes, contains a remarkable collection of the artist's paintings and ceramics.

Since 1977, the undulating wild pine groves in this area have been altered by work on a vast project, entitled Sophia Antipolis, which is intended to become an International City of Wisdom, Science and Technology, engaging in research into a wide range of fields. Modern architecture can already be seen among the woods. Scientists and research-workers from all over the world attend seminars here, seeking the outlines of a future world in an area which has remained unchanged since ancient times.

Above: the old village of Biot, and mural on the front of the Fernand Léger Museum. Opposite: a street in Mougins. Right: brazen construction along the Marina-Baie-des-Anges.

CAGNES AND ITS PAINTERS,
SAINT-PAUL AND ITS POETS

In the middle of the last century, Cros-de-Cagnes was merely a small hamlet where a few fishermen hauled their boats out of the water every morning. Since then a harbor has been built and beaches have been formed: luxury apartment blocks have gone up along the seafront and the race-course has attracted ever increasing numbers of people. Yet beyond Cros, the old roofs of Cagnes still stand, pyramid-like, clustered around the castle which towers over the hill. It was built by the Grimaldi family of Monaco, which chose the protection of the king of France in the 17th century, rather than become a vassal of the Spanish throne. Even so, the Grimaldis were still thrown out at the Revolution and had to take refuge in Nice. Thereafter the fate of the castle fluctuated: having been sold for 8,000 francs in 1875, it was bought in 1939 for 240,000 francs by the city of Cagnes. Its restored rooms contain an

seeking inspiration or a setting for their plots. Jacques Prévert and Marcel Carnet, H.-G. Clouzot, Simone Signoret and Yves Montand were the hosts of the Colombe d'Or. Actually they were merely continuing a tradition as Lamartine, in 1850, had already been to Saint-Paul to inaugurate the village's beautiful fountain!

Some distance from the village, the Maeght Foundation, a center for modern art containing works by Giacometti, Chagal, Miró, Calder and others, blends its modern architecture perfectly with the surrounding pine groves.

One sometimes tends to forget that the French Riviera is the home of the arts. The names of many famous artists are associated with many places within it: Pierre Bonnard with Le Cannet, Picasso with Antibes and Vallauris, Renoir with Cagnes, where Modigliani and Soutine also lived, Matisse and Chagall with Nice, and also Vence, where Marc Chagall lived for many years.

interesting museum of the olive tree and exhibits of modern Mediterranean art.

Cagnes is the city of painters. First of all, Auguste Renoir, who died there in 1919 after spending the last years of his life in the beautiful property of Les Collettes which fortunately has been preserved and has become the Renoir Memorial Museum; its contents include some statues (in the garden), the artist's studio with his wheelchair and materials, and mementoes of his sons Pierre, Jean and Claude. All around are ancient olive trees which, despite their gnarled trunks, bear perpetually new foliage.

From Cagnes the road runs along the bottom of the Malvan Valley to Saint-Paul-de-Vence, a fortified town built on a spur which makes a most impressive sight as one approaches from this direction. The ramparts were built in 1537 on the orders of Francis I, and are more or less intact. The 13th-century church was embellished and adorned with stalls and paintings. Inside it is a narrow street with some very old houses, now used as craft shops and, particularly, as art galleries. Saint-Paul has become famous since so many artists, from the world of literature, painting and the cinema, have descended on it

Left: Cagnes-sur-Mer: general view, medieval castle, Renoir's house, view of les *Baous*. Above: Renoir's "Venus" in the park surrounding the house. Sentry road, St. Paul de Vence. Below: small lane, St. Paul, entrance to the celebrated Auberge de la Colombe d'Or (Golden Dove Inn).

VENCE AND ITS "BAOUS"

In its dominant position at nearly 1,000 ft. above the sea and the valleys, protected from the cold north winds by its *baous* (Alpine foothills), Vence is one of the most attractive of the small towns of the hinterland. Increasing numbers of villas are being built in the surrounding countryside. Even in winter, it is a paradise for perennial flowers and plants: the hillsides are covered with delightful gardens well stocked with mimosas, bougainvilleas, orange trees, almond trees, palms, agaves and rose-laurels.

The old town is enclosed within a ring of lively boulevards and a long well shaded square. There are only a few narrow passages leading into it. Formerly it used to have seven gates; among those that remain, the Peyra Gate opens onto the square of the same name, where there is a splashing fountain. In the heart of the old town are the town hall, the Romanesque cathedral,

Left: St. Paul de Vence. Below: the Maeght Foundation seen from two angles. Below: chapel designed and decorated by Henri Matisse, Vence. Opposite and below: tower of the old castle and fountain at Vence.

which has five naves, Gothic choir stalls and altar pieces of gilded wood. An assortment of souvenirs awaits visitors in the craft and pottery shops which are to be found in the narrow winding streets.

Beyond the Place Thiers, remarkable for its enormous ash tree, the terrace provides one with a fine view of the *baous* and the mountain. A number of chapels are scattered about the surrounding area: the chapels of Sainte-Anne, Saint-Lambert and Sainte-Colombe. But one should not miss the Rosary Chapel, which Matisse decorated with frescoes which are much admired for their purity of line.

To the north there are three roads which make interesting side-trips. One runs towards Saint-Jeannet and Gattières, along high ground overlooking the left bank of the Var. Another climbs six miles to the Vence Pass (3,150 ft.) and crosses desert-type landscapes as far as the mountain hamlets of Coursegoules (3,250 ft.) and Bezaudun (2,600 ft.), both of which are sheltered from the north by the ridges of the Pre-Alps, which rise to 4,875 ft.

Another picturesque road runs westwards along the Loup Valley toward the gorges, passing through Tourrettes-sur-Loup, an astonishing medieval village clinging to the side of a rock face over a sheer drop into the valley.

From the main square the visitor should walk around the narrow streets and inspect the products of the local craftsmen, mainly handweavers and potters, whose work is of a really high standard. The 15th-century church contains a triptych by Bréa and some sculpted altarpieces.

Coursegoules and St. Jeannet *baou*. Below: the medevial village of Tourrettes-sur-Loup.

THE MOUNTAINS OF THE SUN

The topography of the Riviera follows a rather special pattern. To the east of the great gash of the Var Valley, the mountain ranges run parallel to the sea. They rise behind the coastal hills of the Esterel and the Tanneron, forming a first range with the Audibergue, the Haut-Montet and the Puy de Tourettes, which vary in altitude from 3,900 ft. to 5,200 ft. Beyond the high valley of the Loup, there are other even higher ranges: Mount Bleyne, Thorenc and Cheiron, which are also parallel to the Mediterranean, as are the high valleys between them.

To the east of the Var, however, the ranges are at right angles to the coast. This accounts for the difference in appearance and environment between the Grasse and Nice areas.

The upland ranges in the Grasse region are crossed by two rifts, the Nans Valley, and more particularly the Loup Valley, with some splendid gorges which one first comes across at Pont-du-Loup, on the road from Grasse to Vence. While passing the gorges, which stretch for five miles, visitors will note the splendid waterfall and the hermitage of Saint-Arnoux. The astonishing village of Gourdon stands on the ridge of a spur, and is ringed by a terrace with a sheer view down over the valley and the hills, as far as the sea. Between these two rifts, there is an immense desert plateau, crossed by a single road which leads to the village of Caussols. This landscape is pitted with ravines and has practically no vegetation. This is the kind of novelty which most tourists on the Riviera never manage to experience!

Upstream from the Loup Gorges are two old villages: Cipières and Gréolières, each with its old castle and its church with interesting altar pieces. Beyond the ruins of Haut-Gréolières the road crosses a rift and returns to the plateau at Plan de Peyron. A road 6½ miles long leads to the winter-sports resort of Gréolières-les-Neiges, which, like the road, was built some twenty years ago. Just before the road begins its descent one should climb a few yards up the embankment to discover an extraordinary panoramic view of the Esteron Valley and the succession of mountain ranges stretching as far as the Alps. Together with Audibergue, Gréolières-les-Neiges, on the north slope of the Cheiron, is the ski resort closest to Grasse and Cannes. For that very reason it occasionally lacks an adequate snow cover.

At Peyron the road branches off to Thorenc (4,060 ft.), a somewhat neglected climatic resort. However, with its altitude, its fine exposure away from the cold north winds and the pine forests which surround it, Thorenc really has a most healthy climate and is cool in the heat of summer. Bleyne Pass, slightly further up, leads to the Esteron Valley, which is also parallel to the sea, and the villages of Roquestéron, Consegudes and Les Ferres.

Gréolières from two vantage points.

On the basis of documents describing the foundation of a trading post at the mouth of the Paillon, in the 5th century BC, Nice seems to be of Greek origin. The Massaliotes—the Greeks of Marseille—having sailed this far along the coast, settled on the banks of the river, doubtless after first expelling the natives, judging by the name they gave to their settlement: *Nicea,* or Victory.

The city prospered and soon aroused a great deal of envy. Two hundred years later, the Deceates and the Oxybians, who occupied the territory of modern Cannes, became so aggressive that the Massaliotes appealed to their Roman allies for help. An army was sent accordingly, but the Romans took advantage of the invitation in order to settle in the place they were supposed to be defending! Leaving the Greeks on the coast, they occupied the hill known as Cimiez, where they built palaces, an amphitheater and a classical theater. Cimiez thereupon became the aristocratic suburb that it still is today.

Soon after along came the Barbarians, who devastated both the Greek and the Roman cities. It was not long, however, before they reunited and were born again under the guidance of the first

bishops. Nice was still highly coveted, by the counts of Provence, the House of Savoy, the Republic of Genoa and the Kingdom of Sardinia, not to mention the raids by Saracens and pirates and the interplay of princely marriages; as a result of this latter phenomenon, the inhabitants of Nice would wake up one fine morning to discover that they were citizens of Savoy, or France, as the case may be.

Having backed the House of Savoy in the 16th century, Nice was besieged by Francis I, while his ally Barbarossa brought in detachments of Turks. The exploit of Catherine Ségurane, a woman of the people who single-handedly repulsed one group of attackers, gives an idea of the general sentiments of the Niçois. The alliance of the lily and the crescent was short-lived, but France eventually prevailed and Nice added a pearl of great price to the French crown.

Not for long, however! It was returned to Sardinia, and then passed to Spain, and lastly to Piémont. Such was its status when, in 1792, French troops seized it once again. The following year, feeling the breath of the wind of freedom, the people of Nice voluntarily requested to be part of France; Bonaparte made Nice his headquarters for the fight against Sardinia. When the empire collapsed in 1815, Nice reverted to Savoy. Its people, however, clearly yearned for old bonds with France. Fifty years later, the plebiscite proposed by Napoleon III and the king of Italy produced an overwhelming majority in favor of

attachment to France. Nice, a daughter of Marseille, had long been both French and Provençal, in heart and spirit.

By the middle of the 19th century, Nice had already acquired a reputation for charm among the European aristocracy. After the English, the French discovered the allure of a city which was not yet theirs, but was to be soon; for an entire Russian colony, Nice was home for the winter months.

The city began to spread towards the suburb of La Croix-de-Marbre where, on 2 April 1796, Bonaparte had harangued his troops before the

Italian campaign. The Rue de France—so named because it led to the French frontier situated on the Var—then consisted of a few farmhouses and some vegetable gardens. As for the modern Avenue Jean-Médecin, it was an almost impassable dirt road along which the mules traveled on their way to market from the farms of the hinterland. Thereafter, Nice grew in leaps and

Nice. La Promenade des Anglais by day and by night. Opposite and below: Place Masséna.

bounds. While the indigenous population inhabited the winding streets and the Italianate houses of the old town, the winter visitors built themselves luxurious villas on the sea front, at Les Ponchettes, and on the right bank of the Paillon, which the English had made their favorite "promenade".

The people of Nice are very fond of merrymaking, and take every opportunity to indulge in it, to the great delight of foreign visitors eager to savor the picturesque local scene. It was probably during the Second Empire, after the city's return to France, that the Carnival of Nice reached the peak of its brilliance. Its traditions went back to the Middle Ages, and in the 15th century it became sufficiently reputable for the duke of Savoy to come personally to preside over it. In those days it was meant as a celebration for the populace, but it nonetheless provided gentlemen and ladies of distinction with a chance to mingle with the crowd and, their identities concealed by masks, to relish the plainer pleasures of life!

The first *corsi*, involving flower-laden carriages

which the crowds bombarded with bouquets and ribboned candy, took place about 1820. Today, the Carnival of Nice, with its battles of flowers and colorful floats, is still the major attraction of the winter season. It lasts several weeks and preparations keep some people busy all year round. The parade files along the Promenade des Anglais which, in the past century or more, has seen so many kings and princes, artists and poets who had come to the Riviera hoping to find inspiration, rest or an elusive cure. Among its more distinguished guests were two women whose lives were wholly dissimilar. Pauline Bonaparte lived not far from La Croix-de-Marbre, where she gave brilliant receptions, which were to be

Nice. Italian-style façade on an old port building. Landing beneath the arches, Lascaris Palace. Entrance to Hotel Negresco. Right: quaint building known as the "Chateau de l'Anglais" (The Englishman's Castle), the Russian Orthodox church.

followed by even more sophisticated entertaining in 1813-14, when she was living at the Villa Grandis. The whimsical princess came to be known as Our Lady of the Trinkets, and her fantasies sometimes caused quite a stir! On the other hand, Marie Bashkirchev, who had come with her family from Russia, was pursuing a dream. Marie, affectionately known as Moussia, was an artistic soul, who was equally gifted in literature, painting and music. She spent a number of seasons at Nice, hoping to cure the tuberculosis which was oppressing her. She died there, leaving her moving *Diary,* which lays bare her sensitive heart, as well as some canvases which can be seen at the Chéret Museum.

Paradoxically, Nice is a big coastal city without being a major port. It has no large docks and little maritime traffic, except to and from Corsica, for which it is a beach-head on the mainland. And despite some projects currently being elaborated, it seems unlikely that Nice will ever become a big port: its immediate hinterland being mountainous, it lacks any convenient outlet to the interior.

Tourism and the sale of flowers have done so much for its development and are still its main activities. But Nice is also a university and residential city where congresses are frequently held. It is, of course, a major tourist attraction in its own right, besides being an important stopover on the way to Italy and Corsica.

The Promenade des Anglais stretches for about four miles along the Baie des Anges: inland, extensive building has taken place up the sides of the valleys of Magnan-La-Madeleine, St-Barthélémy and Barla, as far as Fabron and La Californie. On the other side of Avenue Jean-Médecin (formerly La Victoire) are the old town and the harbor, at the foot of the castle and Mount Boron. To the north, beyond the Paillon, which is now covered for most of its length, is Cimiez Hill, with its beautiful villas and a cluster of highly interesting sights,

Here we are in the very heart of historic Nice— the Roman city whose amphitheater, thermal

Nice. Left: street in the old town. A cathedral tower. Flower vendor's display. Portside, with the Monument to the Dead in foreground. Following pages: along the quays.

baths and baptistry date back to the early centuries of the Christian era. For the visitor, the vestiges of antiquity still in their original location are supplemented by the archeological museum. Cimiez also has two fairly new museums which make it a favorite with devotees of modern art. The Matisse Museum, which was opened in 1963 with gifts from the artist's family, is housed in the Villa des Arènes. It displays a wide range of the artist's activities—painting, ceramics, engraving—as well as some personal objects from which he derived inspiration, and a number of illustrated books. It becomes evident that Nice and Vence played an important part in Matisse's life.

The Biblical Museum of Marc Chagall, which is even more recent, was specially built to house the gifts made by the artist in 1966 and 1972. These include, in particular, numerous paintings, gouaches, pastels and engraved plates, all on themes of which Chagall once said: "Perfection in art and life flows from biblical sources."

Between Rome and the 20th century, the Renaissance is present with a 15th-century trefoiled cross and a 1662 porch. However, the

neo-Gothic church, which contains works by Bréa, was built in the 19th century.

The Festival of the Gourds has been held every year on the Annunciation for centuries past. Carved and painted pumpkins are sold as receptacles while a jolly party takes place. St-Laurent wine is drunk and the dancing goes on long into the night, when the weather is calm.

From the heights which surround it like the setting of a precious stone, the whole of Nice can be seen facing the perfect arc of the Baie des Anges. Along the waterfront the Promenade des Anglais was laid out in 1822, on the initiative of a cleric from the local English colony. To begin with it was a very ordinary road along the water's edge which gradually became the thoroughfare for fine carriages and an assortment of festivities. Today, between the airport and the Albert I Gardens, it is the liveliest way into town. There are still a number of hotels in the rococo style of the *Belle Epoque,* in amongst the plainer modern shapes: they include the Hôtel Négresco (1912), which has now been declared a classified historical building, and the fine residence, surrounded by gardens, which houses the Musée Masséna. Its luxurious rooms are decorated with paintings, *objets d'art* and period furniture. The nearby Musée Chéret, dedicated to the famous painter and poster artist who died in Nice in 1932, contains canvases from all periods and documents relating the history of the Carnival.

Beyond the Albert I Gardens is the splendid Place Masséna, which is linked by a huge esplanade to Place Garibaldi; both squares have painted arcades and façades, in the Italian style. This is the district of the old casino, the opera house, the modern theater, and, further up, of the Palais des Expositions,

To the east, squeezed between the long thoroughfare which covers the lower reaches of the Paillon and the castle, the old town is a picturesque assembly of narrow streets, stairs and tall houses. The Palais Lascaris, Saint-Jacques church and Sainte-Réparate cathedral (both built in the 17th century), Place Saint-François with its fountain and the old town hall, as well as the Baroque church of Saint-Augustin are all worth a visit.

The famous flower market is still held on the Cours Saley, behind the Ponchettes Galleries, the former arsenal of the Sardinian navy, now occupied by art galleries and restaurants with distinctive local character.

The rock on which the old castle stands separates the old town from the Lympia dock. It is a belvedere, at the foot of which the Rauba Capeu (Niçois for 'stolen hat') leads to the harbor. The castle consists of a few remains and the Tour Bellanda (16th century), which contains the naval museum.

On the other side of the dock, at the foot of Mount Boron, which has now been turned into a park, there is a footpath around the headland, with excellent views of the harbor and waterfront.

The Lower Corniche runs around Mount Boron. It was laid out in the 18th century to facilitate relations between Nice and Italy. The upper Corniche was the work of Napoleon I, who built it using the old *Via Aurelia* from Turbia. The middle Corniche, the most recent, was not finished until 1939. Today it is the most heavily traveled. Each of them makes a most rewarding drive.

Nice. Left: the Roman arena, the Thermae and the monastery at Cimiez Hill. The Massena Museum, Matisse Museum, and Chagall Museum. Above: Mount Boron Observatory. Below: beach scene.

VILLEFRANCHE, LE CAP FERRAT AND BEAULIEU

The delightful port of Villefranche is situated a little further along the coast, well sheltered inside a narrow deep bay. The town was established in the 14th century by Charles II of Anjou, count of Provence and king of Sicily, who granted it commercial freedom *(franchise)*, whence its name. Two centuries later, during the conflict between Francis I and Charles V, Pope Paul II went to Villefranche in an attempt to bring the adversaries together—but to no avail. The citadel of Saint-Elme, the remains of which have been gradually exposed over the past few years, was built about that time.

The charm of Villefranche-sur-Mer lies in its narrow streets sloping, sometimes through dark vaults, down to the sea, in its quaint squares and its brightly colored houses facing the waterfront, where terraced restaurants look out over the harbor and the fishing boats bobbing gently at anchor. Its principal attraction is the Saint-Pierre Chapel, decorated by Jean Cocteau with line frescoes depicting the life of the apostle which combine plainness and beauty.

The nearby beach leads to the Saint-Jean-Cap-Ferrat peninsula. The little town has grown a great deal in recent years, but still preserves its charm. The cape is well served by roads lined for the most part by luxury villas with gardens lushly populated with cypresses, pines, linden trees, etc. The cape has been the home of kings, particularly Leopold II of Belgium, who laid out the *sentier du roy* (king's path) which leads to the lighthouse. Jean Cocteau and Charlie Chaplin were also faithful guests of this select headland. The legacy of Baroness Ephrussi de Rothschild made it possible to build a museum, curiously known as the Ile-de-France, in the *Belle Epoque* style. It contains painting by Tiepolo, Boucher, Fragonard, Renoir and Monet, as well as furniture and tapestries. The grounds of Leopold's former property have been turned into a zoo, with an aquarium, an aviary and a butterfly house.

A path runs round Saint-Hospice Point, at the east of the peninsula. A huge statue of the Virgin stands near the chapel. From the path there are fine views of the whole coastline, as far as the Italian coast.

Beaulieu is situated beyond Saint-Jean, enclosed between the sea and the sheer cliffs of the mountain. Sailing boat enthusiasts flock to the local yachting harbor. At the end of a promontory is Villa Kerylos, quite a faithful reproduction of an ancient Greek villa. It is the work of a dedicated Hellenist, Théodore Reinach. Its interior is decorated and furnished in Greek style. Some authentic objects such as a Cypriot mosaic, are also on display.

Villefranche-sur-Mer: port and inner harbor. Below: St. Jean-Cap-Ferrat. Following pages: private residence at Cape Ferrat.

THE CORNICHES, FROM EZE TO LA TURBIE

Throughout their entire length, the Middle and Upper Corniches provide one with an endless succession of panoramic views and breathtaking vantage points overlooking the capricious shapes of the coast and the towns far below.

Whether the visitor discovers it from the Eze Pass (1,650 ft.) on the Upper Corniche, or around a bend in the Middle Corniche, the village of Eze commands admiration by virtue of its position on a rocky spur above a fairly sheer drop towards the sea. Its castle was demolished on the orders of Louis XIV, but this eagle's nest still makes an impressive sight, and simply must be visited. Visitors will be rewarded for their efforts by the sight of ancient narrow streets intersected by vaulted passages, luxuriously restored old houses and craft shops. A tropical garden has been planted on the land near the site of the original

castle. A steep footpath leads down from the village to Eze-sur-Mer, at the foot of the rock.

The other side of the Eze Pass is La Turbie, a belvedere which is famous for its Augustan Trophy, built in the year 5 BC. It recorded the triumph of the emperor "over the Alpine peoples, from the Upper Sea (the Adriatic) to the Lower Sea (the Mediterranean) which are subject to the Roman Empire"—to quote the words of the inscription carved on its plinth. The Augustan Trophy, which has been damaged over the centuries, was restored in the early part of this century. A small museum contains a model of the monument in its original condition. The village church dates from the 18th century and contains some beautiful works by Veronese, Ribera, Van Loo and Bréa. At 1,560 ft., La Turbie towers over the Principality of Monaco which can be reached by a road consisting largely of hairpin bends. Another fine road, which runs around the Tête de Chien, sweeps down towards Cap d'Ail.

From Nice it is possible to get to La Turbie along an inland road which climbs the Laghet Valley towards the sanctuary of Our Lady of Laghet. The sanctuary contains a most remarkable collection of votive offerings, the sight of which prompted the poet Guillaume Apollinaire to say: "Even those who have no faith will be touched by the painstaking attention to detail and the utter lack of sophistication of this primitive art, and by the sense of wonderment which must have inspired its authors."

The Madonna to whom the miracles evoked by these votive offerings are attributed is clad in white satin embroidered in gold. Even today the Madonna is highly venerated.

Left: overall view of Cape Ferrat and gardens. Below: Beaulieu Port. Above: Eze and the tropical gardens. Below: memorial plaque and the Augustan Trophy, La Turbie.

MONACO

The date of the earliest settlements in the Monaco area is lost in the mists of time. Rock shelters have been discovered near the oceanographic museum, and the Grimaldi Caves, near Menton, have brought to light a human type which seems closely related to Cro-Magnon Man, though having more pronounced negroid traits. These finds belong to the upper paleolithic age, some 30,000 to 40,000 years before the birth of Christ.

The Phenicians were the first occupants of the area in historical times. They built a temple to their god Melkarth (Hercules), whence the name Portus Herculis Monoeci which occurs later, during the Roman occupation. The barbarian invasions, from both the north and the sea, ruined the trading posts along the coast. By the Middle Ages, Port Hercules was nothing more than a fishing village.

In the 12th century, however, the Republic of Genoa obtained the territory from Emperor Frederick I, and built a fortress there in 1215. Thereafter, Monaco was to share the fate of the Genovese. Having been coveted by both the Guelphs and the Ghibellines, it became the fief of a member of the Grimaldi family in 1297, but was still the subject of frequent struggles. It was taken by Charles I, but then bought back by the Grimaldis, an important family which had several branches in the region and which was to give its name and coat-of-arms to the lords of Monaco. Indeed, the history of the city is linked to that of the family.

The Grimaldis were no angels: greed for power sometimes drove them to commit crimes, with brothers and nephews killing each other in

attempts to secure the protection of a powerful neighbor, France or Spain, thereby consolidating their position. In 1792 the arrival of the French army on the banks of the Var led the people of Monaco to constitute a republic and request union with France. This was confirmed by a decree of 15 February 1793, incorporating the principality into the *département* of Alpes-Maritimes.

Through the intervention of Talleyrand, the

Matignon-Grimaldi family recovered sovereignty over the principality in 1814. But the fall of the empire cost France its protectorate, which was ceded to Sardinia. In 1814, tiring of the punitive taxation imposed by the government, Menton and Roquebrune—which were then a part of the principality—declared themselves free towns; in 1860, after the death of their president, the inhabitants voted to become part of France, at the

Monaco. Entrance to Prince's Palace. Full view of palace. Regal windows perched atop the rock. Below and right: port and gardens.

same time as the annexation of Nice.

This left the principality in a reduced state, consisting of Monaco alone. The Spélugues Plateau, on which Monte-Carlo was to be built, was still covered with olive and orange trees. Twenty years later, a new town had been built there—one to which the European upper classes were soon to flock, in pursuit of pleasure!

Today the principality consists of two very different towns, separated by La Condamine harbor. South of the harbor is the old town of Monaco, built on its rocky platform. The new town of Monte-Carlo, which is only one hundred years old, is spread out to the north, up as far as the slopes of Beausoleil: as it could not reach out horizontally, it has tended to grow upwards, with tall modern apartment blocks.

The images of these two places could hardly be

more dissimilar—and the same could be said, more or less, of their visitors! The international tourists wait outside the Palace for the daily Changing of the Guard, while the other side of the harbor the vast and eager gambling fraternity moves in on the green baize tables of the Casino and the big hotels! With such throngs of visitors each year, the principality lives and thrives, to the point where it must be begging the sea to retreat to make room for more land!

In Monaco the road climbs from the harbor to the Place du Palais. The palace itself was originally built in the thirteenth century, but the south façade, which looks over the square, is in the Italian Renaissance style. The Court of Honor, with its arcaded galleries, is of a later period; it is adorned with 16th- and 17th- century frescoes. The throne room and the state apartments are 19th century. This is the residence of the prince and his family, who are protected by the palace guard, with their fine uniforms, and by the *carabiniers,* whose barracks, in the 18th century Genovese style, face the palace.

From the terrace, which is adorned with cannons which were a gift from Louis XIV, there is a majestic view of the harbor, Monte-Carlo and the steep mountains which tower over the entire

scene. The oceanographic museum, which is one of the most complete in the world, lies a short distance away, through the narrow streets of the old town. It was founded in 1910 by Prince Albert I of Monaco, himself an expert oceanographer and a dedicated man of the sea. Besides some models of the yachts and the whaling ship in which he sailed the oceans, the museum contains several magnificent aquariums in which brightly colored fish swim among marine flora, and also a number of whale skeletons, fishing equipment, marine instruments and much more. It is a living encyclopedia of the sea. The museum is surrounded by terraced gardens which look down over the Mediterranean from nearly 200 feet.

Another prince, Charles III, created the gambling resort of Monte-Carlo. The Casino built by Charles Garnier, the architect of the Paris Opera House, is a masterpiece of the *Belle Epoque* style, with its gaming rooms, theater, bars and plush decor. At the bottom of the terrace, just above the sea, a new Congress Center has been built in recent years. Artificial beaches, luxury pools, aristocratic sporting club—this Mecca of gambling is also a place of pleasure where the privileged élite of the modern West—and the new Orient—now meet!

Monte Carlo. A town "on the rise". Above: the famous Monte Carlo Casino.

This area begins very close to the town, with the hills which ring the chief built-up area, and the peaks visible on the horizon: Mount Boron, Mount Gros with its observatory, and Mount Chauve. The valleys which separate them fan out towards the upland areas. These rocky slopes, which are open to the sea winds, steep and dried out by the sun, are often arid and covered with brush which is occasionally destroyed by fires. One of the most charming features of the Nice hinterland is the perched villages which can be seen in many places clinging to rocky outcrops on the sides of mountains.

Falicon, the closest of these, looks down over a vast expanse of olive groves and croplands. Behind it are the Saint-André Grotto and the ruins of Saint-Pons Abbey. There are two amazing villages a little to the east, further up the Paillon valley: Peille, on the side of Mount Baudon, a medieval village with an arcaded

square, a Gothic-Romanesque church and a maze of streets; and Peillon, perched on a rocky spur, in a most extraordinary position.

Several roads run north from the valleys of the Var and the Paillon to the villages of Aspremont, Tourrettes-Levens, Levens, Contes, Berre-les-Alpes and L'Escarène, where a number of roads meet. The villages are linked by two main passes: Saint-Roch and Braus (nearly 3,250 ft).

Steep and virtually inaccessible slopes separate the valleys. Yet these villages are definitely worth a visit, for the beauty of their churches, the remarkable views which they provide and for their generally picturesque charm. Coaraze has a number of ceramic sundials, including one signed by Jean Cocteau. Lucéram, the upper part of which clings to the mountain, has a fine church with some interesting altarpieces, a ruined castle and some old Gothic houses. A series of impressive hairpin bends takes one to Peira Cava (5,135 ft), a summer and winter resort town, a superb balcony overlooking the Riviera and the Alps. The same road runs horizontally, to Turini, through a forest of pine, larch and beech. Eventually it comes to L'Aution, at more than 3,500 ft., opposite the Cime du Diable.

Braus Pass joins the Bévera Valley at Sospel, a small town in the hollow of a lush basin, noted for its coolness in summer. The old bridge, which had been destroyed in 1944, has been rebuilt. The town's attractions comprise the church of Saint-Michel (1641), the ruins of a convent and a corner tower of the old ramparts.

As we can see, the Nice hinterland is made up of picturesque villages and mountain sites which are a prelude to the nearby upland valleys.

Falicon and Peille. Opposite: a street in Sospel. Right: Entrevaux.

THE THREE VALLEYS

The Var, a capricious river with a great many banks of pebbles along its course, flows into the sea west of Nice, near the airport. Some 15 miles upstream the valley narrows abruptly at the Chaudan Defile, and then forks to the west, parallel to the ranges of hills in the hinterland above Grasse. Its upper reaches resume a north-south direction, as do the left-bank tributaries, the Cians, the Tinée and the Vésubie, whose upland valleys extend as far as the frontier range.

Nice thus provides access to some extraordinarily beautiful and varied mountain scenery which is perhaps not as well known as one would expect it to be. In order even to list its many attractions we would have to fill an inordinately large part of this book; so we shall confine ourselves to a description of the course of the valleys flowing into the Baie des Anges. First and foremost, of course, the one which carries them all down to the

sea: the Var, which since 1860 has had the curious distinction of flowing throughout its entire length in Alpes-Maritimes, and not in the *département* which bears its name!

The Var rises at 5,550 ft. in an Alpine grazing area just below the Cayole Pass. A thin line of water runs along through the stones and then cascades down into the Sanguinière Torrent, a larger stream which is, however, formed solely from melting snow. There are a number of chalets in the midst of the pastures, facing the Aiguilles de Pelens... The road follows the torrent, which is intersected by paths of fallen stone at the foot of sheer rock faces. Then we come to the first villages: Entraunes and then Saint-Martin d'Entraunes, which has a church with an early Gothic porch and a fine altarpiece by François Bréa. The roofing of the houses is wooden, but the tall colored façades and iron balconies of the Nice area are already much in evidence. Some way beyond Villeneuve d'Entraunes, roofs of round

tiles are a clear sign of the approach of Provence, with cherry trees, fig trees and vines—and, on summer days, the chirping of crickets!

The ruins of a castle look down over the small resort of Guillaumes, at the junction with the road to the Valberg Pass. Shortly thereafter the valley narrows between the reddish slopes which precede the Daluis Gorges. These run for about five miles, carving a savage gash in the mountain as well as some rock faces and other formations which have the strangest shapes. Between the tunnels, the road runs about three hundred feet above the river. Suddenly, after a bend in the road, the valley widens again, and its waters spread out among the banks of pebbles which lie along its bed all the way to the sea.

There are a number of old towns along the river banks. They include Entrevaux, which was fortified by Vauban, has a citadel which looks down over the round towers of its principal gateway; Puget-Théniers, a city of the Templars,

which has a church with some beautiful carved wood; Touët-sur-Var, clinging to the rocky slope; Villars-sur-Var, and others. Plan-du-Var marks the point at which the wider lower valley begins.

A mile and a half from Touët the Var is joined by the Cians, which flows down from the foothills of Mount Mounier (9,350 ft), the giant of this Alpine region. An extremely picturesque road climbs up the valley through the Cians Gorges, a well known tourist route usually connected, via Beuil and Valberg, with the trip through the Deluis Gorges. In as little as 15 miles, the Cians drops 5,200 ft: it is easy to imagine the dramatic appearance of the gorges through which it has forced its way!

The lower part, with the splendid Thiéry Waterfall, consists of grey rocks on fairly green slopes. Higher up, towards the Great Rift (La Grande Clue), the Passage de l'Enfer, the road passes close to stalactites of ice; the ground here is frequently covered with black ice.

At 4,875 ft the road enters Beuil, which from the 14th to the 17th centuries was the fief of the Grimaldi family and was coveted by both Savoy and France. All that remains of its past is the White Penitents' Chapel, which was built with the stones of the castle. Roads from this well-situated mountain village lead to the valleys of the Tinée and the Var, the latter via Valberg, four miles away, which is both a winter and summer resort. As it is located on a pass facing the nearby mountain ranges, some beautiful Alpine pastures and pine groves, it is a useful starting point for some rewarding side-trips into the smaller valleys, and particularly to Péone, an out-of-the-way

village, and the valley of Aygue-Blanchè.

A very winding road leads from Beuil to Saint-Sauveur-de-Tinée, on the road from Nice to Auron, and to Isola 2000, the large skiing centers in Alpes-Maritimes.

At 5,225 ft Auron is a fine resort which has kept much of its original character as an Alpine village. There are ski lifts to Las Donnas, (7,330 ft) which being located on a plateau is assured of excellent exposure to the sun. The road from Auron to St-Etienne-de-Tinée runs through some lovely pine groves, opposite the peaks of the frontier range.

From the village of Isola, a difficult, and occasionally impassable road climbs to Isola 2000, at the foot of the Lombarde Pass into Italy.

Isola 2000 was founded about twelve years ago. Its block-like clusters of buildings contain hotels, cafés, shops and other facilities. A cable car runs to the Tête de Pélevos (8,190 ft). The numerous ski runs are very well laid out.

Valberg Forest and a glimpse of Beuil. Right: snow at Auron, and St. Etienne-de-Timée Village.

The Vésubie Valley is another beautiful way to reach the higher mountain areas. It joins the Var at Plan-du-Var, and, soon after the Durandy Bridge, enters a stretch of impressive gorges with partly wooded sheer walls. Frenchmen's Leap (Saut des Français) is the point at which, according to tradition, Republican soldiers were tossed into the void below by bands of Nice guerrillas in 1793. Slightly upstream from there, at Saint-Jean-la-Rivière, a bridge crosses the Vésubie. A series of hairpin bends runs up through some splendid olive groves to Utelle, a large village at 2,600 ft, where there are some ruined ramparts and the church of Saint-Véran, which has a remarkable *Annunciation* of the 15th-century Nice school. Another road, of even more forbidding appearance, leads to the Madonna of Utelle, which was once a famous sanctuary; the view of the surrounding mountains is well worth the climb.

Beyond Saint-Jean-la-Rivière the valley broadens before we come to Lantosque, which is perched on a rocky outcrop, then La Bollène-Vésubie—by another road—and lastly Roquebillière and Belvédère, on either side of the river.

This region of pastures, pine groves and mountain springs is known as the Switzerland of Nice. It provides endless opportunities for hiking and climbing, towards the Estrech Waterfall along the Gordolasque Valley and towards La Foux, with its man-made lakes and its amphitheater of mountains. The Nice shelter, at 7,254 ft, is a base for the ascent of Mount Clapier and Le Gelas, whose ridges of nearly 10,000 ft mark the Italian frontier.

Other trips may be made from Saint-Martin-Vésubie, the last village in the valley, at 3,120 ft. This quite popular resort has some interesting old houses, a White Penitents' Chapel, and a church with its original 17th-century decoration intact, a Madonna dressed in lace and an altarpiece attributed to Louis Bréa. There are two paved roads beyond Saint-Martin: one of them goes to the Madonna of Fenestre, near a shelter of the French Alpine Club, and the other to the Boréon Waterfall, at the end of a small dammed lake, in a setting highly reminiscent of the Tyrol.

This brings us to the foot of the Mercantour Natural Park, along the Italian frontier: it is a paradise for mountain-climbers and also for the chamois and the ibex which roam through the forests and along the rocky slopes of this vast unspoilt domain.

La Bollène-Vésubie: village street. Right: flowers and moufflan, a variety of long-horn sheep, in Mercantour National Park. Following pages: the "Switzerland of Nice".

ROQUEBRUNE

Situated between Monte Carlo and Menton, Roquebrune and Cape Martin provide two points of interest for casual tourists or for those with a penchant for history.

Roquebrune is particularly noteworthy because of its castle, which was what actually gave rise to the town. It was built by Count de Vintimille in the 10th century and originally served as a mere gaol—a defense outpost against Sarrazin incursion. In the 15th century the Grimaldi family ordered further construction to bolster the ramparts and provide quarters for soldiers and their families. Thus the village came into being with its old houses that can still be seen banked up against the hill.

Steep, narrow streets lead to the keep, which contains vaulted rooms, a contemporary kitchen and a small local museum. From the upper platform there is a fine view over the coast and Cap Martin, with its villas and olive groves.

Every year, on Good Friday and 5 August, processions are held at Roquebrune. Their theme is the Passion of Christ, and they were instituted in response to a wish expressed in 1467, during an epidemic of the plague in the region.

Cap Martin is a residential area. A footpath runs around the edge of the peninsula, through a landscape where nature is still master!

A number of narrow roads climb from the coast to the highland areas around Gorbio and Sainte-Agnès, two villages which enjoy a superb location on the side of a mountain. The approaches to Sainte-Agnès are even more striking, coming from Peille along a corniche which runs around Mount Baudon, through a landscape of savage grandeur.

Further up into the mountains, the road from Sospel via the Castillon Pass crosses the village of the same name which was devastated in the war. On the other side of the valley, Castellar, laid out in terraces, is about six miles from Menton.

MENTON AND THE LEGEND
OF THE LEMON TREE

Menton, the town situated on the Italian frontier, is, according to Maupassant, the warmest and the healthiest of the towns in which to spend the winter—at a time when it was highly

fashionable to spend the winters on the Riviera. Lord Byron went even further, speaking of "this land which brings Paradise to one's mind". In fact his sentiments are borne out by an ancient legend whereby, when Adam and Eve were expelled from Paradise on Earth—which could not have been far away!—the fair-haired Eve stole a lemon which she hid in her hair. Once she had reached the region of Menton with her companion and had been overwhelmed by the beauty of the place, she threw the lemon on the ground, saying: "Grow and multiply, Oh fruit of Heaven, in this land which is worthy of you!" And the nearby slopes were soon covered with trees bearing golden fruit.

Left: two views of Roquebrune. Above and below: assorted scenes from Menton.

For centuries past, each year in February, the Lemon Festival has taken place admidst general merrymaking.

If this legend is merely a fable, then it must have been thought up by a poet. Another poet— Jean Cocteau—is present here: he decorated the wedding room in the town hall and, down near the harbor, has his own small museum, the façade of which is adorned with a pebble mosaic modeled on a drawing by the poet.

This old Italian-style town is also a center for the arts. The Menton Biennale provides a panorama of contemporary painting in the Palais de l'Europe, and every summer a Music Festival is held in the open air in the marvelous setting of Place Saint-Michel, next to the 17th-century Baroque church of Saint-Michel and the White Penitents' Chapel. In the words of Jean Cocteau: "See the magic of the opera: its lights are stars, the boxes are bedrooms, the staircase is made of moon and candelabras, and its silence is made of the faint rumbling of streets and waves".

Beyond this terraced square, which is reached by a double staircase, lies the old town with its vaulted passageways, its centuries-old houses and its cold shade. Higher up again is the curious cemetery with four terraces, each of which is reserved for the dead of a different religion, and the Jardin des Colombières, which contains box trees, cypresses and succulent plants.

Menton also reminds one of Katherine Mansfield. The novelist's friends bought the villa known as *Isola Bella*, to serve as a museum honoring the memory of that young woman who went to Menton searching for a hopeless cure. She died two years later at Fontainebleau at the age of thirty-two.

Menton: the town hall, the Jean Cocteau Museum, and the route de l'Annonciade. Right: view of the Old Town. Following pages: le Lac Vert (Green Lake)in, the Région des Merveilles.

THE UPPER ROYA VALLEY

Natural boundaries have also been known to undergo political fluctuations! The frontier between France and Italy should run along the dividing line in the middle of the watercourse; but for nearly a century this was not so. The 1860 treaty whereby Savoy and the countship of Nice were attached to France contained a special clause ceding to Italy the French slope of the Alpes Maritimes in the region of Mercantour, this being a hunting area of which the king of Italy was particularly fond. Out of courtesy Napoleon accepted this anomaly—whereupon Tende and La Brigue found themselves annexed by Italy.

It was not until after the Second World War, in the Peace Treaty signed with Italy on 15 September 1947, that this privilege came to an end. France thus recovered the upper valleys of the Tinée, the Vésubie and the Roya, as well as Tende and La Brigue.

Both rail and road then ascend the course of the river, leaving the village of Saorge, with its houses spread out on the side of the mountain. The church of the Madonna del Poggio, which has a Lombard belltower, contains some 15th-century frescoes. The valley then broadens towards Fontan, before narrowing once more as it enters the Bergue Gorges which extend until Saint-

Dalmas-de-Tende, where it meets two other valleys: the Levense, which leads to La Brigue and Notre-Dame-des-Fontaines, a modest chapel with some remarkable frescoes of the life of Christ.

In the opposite direction, the Minière Valley goes deep into the mountain. The road reaches a dead end at Mesches Lake. The only way into the appropriately named Vallée des Merveilles (Valley of the Marvels), at the foot of Mount Bego (9,324 ft) is along a footpath. Some mysterious signs are to be seen carved in the schist rock; they were discovered as far back as the 17th century, but were then neglected for two centuries. It was not until the end of the 19th century that an English scholar decided to study them; to facilitate his research, he built a house on the spot. He counted more than 36,000 carvings, the origin of which, though still uncertain, appears to be prehistoric.

The old houses of the mountain town of Tende, their roofs covered with flat stones, are laid out like an amphitheater above the Roya. All that remains of Lascaris Castle is a single erect wall pointing skywards. The old church, in the Lombard style, has a square belltower.

This is the last French town before the frontier, 5 miles away; the Tende Pass leads through a tunnel into Italy, towards the winter resort of Limone.

Two views of the Lac Vert. Tende. Right: View of the summits of Valberg. Cyprus Gardens, cactus and other succulent plants. Menton. Last page: sunset over the Bay of Angels.